I0483215

# The *Art* of Storytelling

## AN IMPACTFUL TOOL FOR CHANGE IN TODAY'S WORK ENVIRONMENT

**AN IMPACTFUL TOOL FOR CHANGE IN TODAY'S WORK ENVIRONMENT**

# Dr. Radisha Brown

Copyright ©2018

By Dr. Radisha Brown

All rights reserved. No part of this book may be produced or transmitted in any form or any means, electronic or mechanical, including photocopying, recording, or by information storage and retrieval system, without written permission from Dr. Radisha Brown, personal.

*Formatted and Designed by Amy D. Kilpatrick, www.Designworxs.net*

Dr. Radisha Brown
125 Commercial Blvd
PO Box 211317
Martinez, GA 30917
Email: DrRadisha@gmail.com

ISBN-10:    16-4254-3608
ISBN-13:    97-8164254-3605

ISBN 9781642543605   $14.95
51495

9 781642 543605

# FROM THE AUTHOR

Organizational stories were studied as a means for key messages and values to travel rapidly across organizational boundaries, focusing on how resilience and adaptive organizational behavior occur during times of uncertainty and great change.

Conceptually, the dissertation bridges the literature of contemporary leadership, storytelling, and organizational commitment to provide a clearer understanding of how stories contribute to strategic organizational change. The relevant contemporary leadership, organizational identity, commitment, and resilience, and organizational storytelling literature are discussed and integrated within the context of turbulent economic forces. The ways in which meaning and values are conveyed, particularly through stories within organizations, under these conditions are presented and articulated as key conceptual linkages for this research. A qualitative research approach was employed by interviewing nine participants from different industries in the United States serving as the primary data set.

Through storytelling, leaders and organizational members convey core values and make sense out of complex internal and external messages more effectively, displaying enhanced commitment and resilience, even during turbulent times; these are essential capabilities in light of changing career and organizational dynamics.

# DEDICATION

This book is dedicated to anyone that ever felt invisible and unloved as I once felt. Despite the obstacles in life you are one of a kind as God only made one of you because you are perfect!

I owe many thanks to my loving family and dear friends who encouraged me to make my dream a reality. I would like to thank my mother, Loretta Brown, and father, Alfred Bernard Wright, because without them meeting, I would not be here to enjoy this great accomplishment. I would like to thank My foster parents, Karen and Alan Morton, because they encouraged me to further my education. I would like to thank the many strangers that have provided encouraging words on the days that I struggled to find purpose. I would like to Thank Jesus Christ who carried me through many difficult days.

This book is dedicated to all strong and courageous women; especially my grandmothers, Bessie Mae Freeman, Flossie Wright because I stand on the foundation of their sacrifices.

# CONTENTS

# The Art of Storytelling

AN IMPACTFUL TOOL FOR CHANGE IN TODAY'S WORK ENVIRONMENT

# INTRODUCTION

Gaining the support of an organization's members is one of the most important functions of effective management. Organizational executives are symbolic figures, and their communication is typically representative and intertwined with the company image, values, and beliefs. This dissertation explores the use of leadership (management) communication as a strategic tool to prompt organizational identity change among internal stakeholders.

Recent studies have suggested that organizational storytelling is an effective method of transmitting values, sharing knowledge, building cohesion, and garnering support and action of internal stakeholders (Adamson, Pine, Van Steenhoven, & Kroupa, 2006; Cullen, 2008; Denning, 2010). Storytelling is a humanistic approach that engages the listener to partake in the story, embody the protagonist and interpret the story through his or her own lens. Furthermore, storytelling builds on the emotional and cognitive aspects of the human condition to establish a relational dynamic between storyteller and listener. Communication as a leadership strategy is a recent phenomenon within organizations (Denning, 2010).

# STRUCTURE OF THE DISSERTATION

This dissertation explored the topic of using storytelling as a communication tool for organizational change.

- **Section One** introduces the topic of storytelling by presenting background, purpose and research questions of the study.

- **Section Two** presents a review of relevant literature, highlighting the previous research carried out in this field. It provides a study of previous work, which was carried out in related fields, and gives specific research related to a wide spectrum of thought on the topic of using storytelling as a communication tool for organizational change.

- **Section Three** explains the methodology for data collection.

- **Section Four** presents the findings.

- **Section Five** concludes with a discussion, recommendations, and future research.

Dr. Radisha Brown

The Art of Storytelling

# Problem Background

# Telling the Story

What messages do we transmit in the stories we tell? What characteristics do the stories reveal about the storytellers? What can we learn about the organizations of which we are members by the way we describe our experiences? And, finally, how well are the leadership messages being passed on through our organizations?

These are the types of questions that have led me to this point in my research on leadership and organizational change. Leaders today wrestle with massive operational and strategic challenges to attempt to unify their organizations to compete more effectively in today's complex global competitive marketplace. Stories are continually told by leaders and followers about the passages and trials that they and their organizations have faced.

These organizational stories, in fact, often serve as a conduit to deliver, and receive, essential messages about the strategic direction and well-being of organizations and their members. In the past, much research in this area focused on organizational storytelling primarily as a function of organizational commitment and culture: One's commitment to the organization grew over time along

Dr. Radisha Brown

with an increasing sense of identity to and within the organization.

Narrating was seen in a larger extent in an anthropological sense, where constituent components were connected through continuous and managed contact among longer-term and more senior employees, listening to stories about hierarchical life and deliberately watching authoritative practices and customs. The latter created an emergent thankfulness for hierarchical standards and values.

A potent and convenient line of research asked whether, given the developing nature of professions today (where authoritative participation quickly changes, determined by assorted vocational ways and uniquely abbreviated residencies inside individual associations) and dynamic hierarchical motion (wherein associations are progressively combined, scattered, virtual, and unstructured), stories played a fundamental role communicating the change procedure.

When associations and their employees undergo rapid change, how do internal stakeholders efficiently establish how to perform their role in the face of expanding vulnerability and equivocation? The current authoritative scene requires versatility, whereby internal stakeholders can persevere through progressively perplexing and oft- times troublesome circumstances. Pioneers and hierarchical parts, regardless of abbreviated residency inside every association, must have the capacity to react more quickly and adequately to turbulent conditions and changing business sector strengths.

Fundamentally, stories facilitate the sense-making process in The Art of Storytelling these settings, serving a vital - and potentially essential - role for adaptation and strategic change. Listening to and studying organizational stories more carefully brings about a richer understanding of organizations and leadership in the contemporary turbulent business environment.

In sum, the research here broadly seeks to provide the following:

- Insight into how stories impact individuals in organizations during times of change

- Evidence of how storytelling influences organizational commitment, resilience and core values to build identity and adaptability

- Confirm or disconfirm the importance of organizational stories, despite (or perhaps because of) the changing nature of organizations and careers today

- Confirm or disconfirm that storytelling is an integral part of leadership at all organizational levels

# Dissertation Overview

This dissertation, therefore, explores the phenomenon of *organizational storytelling*, where stories serve to convey meaning and to pass on values in organizations, linking the organization's members more tightly with one another and their leaders.

A particularly important aspect of this research is the role and impact of stories as a way for organizational members to rapidly establish common values as a unifying framework to withstand turbulence and change, to build organizational commitment and

Dr. Radisha Brown

resiliency, and to do so even under shortened tenure cycles within individual organizations.

Fundamentally, the values or value system of beliefs and guiding principles, held by members are the glue that binds the organization more closely during periods of uncertainty and change. An important aspect of this dissertation is the examination of the consistency of values expressed across organizational members in this scenario; the research investigates the linkages between existing, stated organizational values and the themes embedded in stories told about past and present periods of organizational change.

Furthermore, the specific role that stories play in promoting organizational commitment and resiliency is studied and tested, offering key insights into contemporary organizational life, where change is more frequent and unpredictable than in the past. To this end, the primary research question driving this dissertation is, "How do organizational stories contribute to organizational commitment and resilience to facilitate adaptation and the successful management of change?" The degree of value congruency and evidence of resiliency found across organizational members was analyzed for varying properties of identity and organizational commitment.

Findings shed valuable light upon understanding how leaderships' messages and practices come together to instill adaptive organizational behavior, the capacity for organizational members to work together and change in concert with difficulties, uncertainty, and dynamic market forces while rapidly moving toward strategic objectives. It is widely acknowledged that telling stories is a vital part

The Art of Storytelling

of the construction of meaning and understanding in social situations, particularly for leaders.

This dissertation builds on previous research on organizational storytelling as a way for members to establish common values and strengthen identity as a unifying framework to respond to difficult situations or times of great change. The study links several major theoretical frameworks under contemporary conditions (leadership and organizational storytelling as well as organizational identity, commitment, and resilience), providing an integrative lens through which to view the conceptual framework that serves as its foundation. This integration makes a significant contribution.

Furthermore, this study provides a detailed description of how stories convey organizational values, and thus offers a clearer understanding of how organizational commitment and resiliency are built during times of great change.

# Background of the Study

In the contemporary business environment, storytelling has emerged as an effective communication tool for organizational change. In the dynamic and competitive global environment, organizational change has become highly important for achieving survival and growth. According to Harris and Barnes (2006), sharing experiences through stories creates a strong relationship between leaders and subordinates in an organization.

The exchange of knowledge and values through stories increases mutual understanding that brings about organizational

Dr. Radisha Brown

change. Human resource in the organization needs to be influenced and persuaded towards a positive organizational change.

Storytelling is one of the most powerful and effective communication tools because it enhances trust, knowledge, learning and emotional connections (Barker & Gower, 2010). Organizational change can be achieved by influencing people to respond positively and willingly. Effective communication tools need to be used by organizations to develop a strong bond with employees.

Among different communication tools, storytelling has emerged in the wake of recognizing the value of human resource management. It is imperative to understand that human resource is the key assets of an organization and, without effective human resource management, organizational change cannot be achieved. Organizational change is required to improve the performance and practices of the organization to meet the changing demands of the competitive markets.

Therefore, using the effective communication tool that is found in storytelling can help achieve successful organizational change with minimal resistance to the change.

# Purpose of the Study

This dissertation offers a unique perspective - theoretically and methodologically - on the analysis of organizational storytelling. The organizational story is typically the sole focus of academic and professional analysis, in which it is treated as a static entity. This detracts, however, from the underlying meaning of the message when communication is integrally linked to the message that precedes or follows it.

The analysis should account for the entire message communicated to internal stakeholders, which consists of the story and communications that accompany a story (preceding or proceeding message), thus becoming a "storytelling event." This dissertation explored the extent to which storytelling event participants experienced promotion of their identification when the organization was undergoing an identity transformation.

Thus, the research question to help understand this dynamic was: How can a leadership 'storytelling event' prompt organizational identity change amongst internal stakeholders? The dissertation incorporated organizational identity and sense-making theories to provide insight into the storytelling event dynamics. Listening to a

Dr. Radisha Brown

story is a self-referential process.

Hence, exploration of the rhetoric that prompts identification within the storytelling event is a worthy endeavor. Internal stakeholder adoption of an organizational identity results in decision making that benefits the organization.

# The Rationale of the Study

This study assessed storytelling as a communication tool for organizational change. The need for storytelling as a communication tool for organizational change has become an important topic due to the increasing problems faced during organizational change. According to Karkabi, Wald, and Castel (2013), organizational change is perceived negatively by the stakeholders of the organization, especially internal stakeholders.

The internal stakeholders of the organization who mainly perceive change as negative are employees. Yet without employee engagement, change cannot be achieved positively. It is, therefore, crucial to study and analyze innovative and effective communication tools that can be used to minimize negative perceptions and attitudes of employees towards organizational change.

The study assessed the significance of storytelling, which can be used to inspire and motivate employees towards organizational change. Employee engagement and commitment can be enhanced by using storytelling as a communication tool (Mittins, Abratt & Christie, 2011).

The Art of Storytelling

In the contemporary business environment, it becomes imperative to analyze communication tools and management practices that enhance the motivation and engagement of stakeholders towards organizational change. The role of storytelling as a communication tool needs to be assessed through various aspects to achieve positive organizational change.

Dr. Radisha Brown

The Art of Storytelling

CHAPTER

3

# Research Questions

There were two research questions. One, what is the significance of storytelling as a communication tool for organizational change? Two, what is the relationship between storytelling as a communication tool and organizational change?

The aim of the study was to examine the use of storytelling as a communication tool for organizational change. Its main objectives were:

- To understand the concept of storytelling as a communication tool for organizational change.

- To assess the significance of storytelling as a communication tool for organizational change.

- To identify the kinds of contexts in which storytelling as a communication tool is useful for achieving organizational change.

- To analyze the role of storytelling as a communication tool for organizational change.

Dr. Radisha Brown

The Art of Storytelling

# The Significance of the Study

Because organizations face intense competition and complexities, this study is significant to the contemporary business environment. It has become imperative that organizations develop innovative and effective communication tools for achieving positive organizational change. Organizational change is needed when environmental factors put pressure on the organization to be flexible and responsive to new demands.

Organizational change and communication have a strong relationship to achieving the objectives of the organization. Additionally, it is imperative to understand that communication is the cornerstone of management practices and communication tools that influence the behavior and attitude of stakeholders.

The most important stakeholders of the organization are employees and customers. For achieving organizational change, the internal stakeholders (who are the employees) need to be convinced of the need to be adaptive and flexible about organizational change.

This study examined the role of storytelling as a communication tool for organizational change. The understanding of storytelling as an effective communication tool is important to achieve positive organizational change and transformation. This

Dr. Radisha Brown

study also identified the kinds of contexts in which storytelling is useful for achieving organizational change.

Finally, the research findings highlight the significance of storytelling as a change agent and communication tool for organizational change. The role of storytelling was analyzed for paving the way for a positive organizational change.

Figure 1 illustrates the conceptual framework.

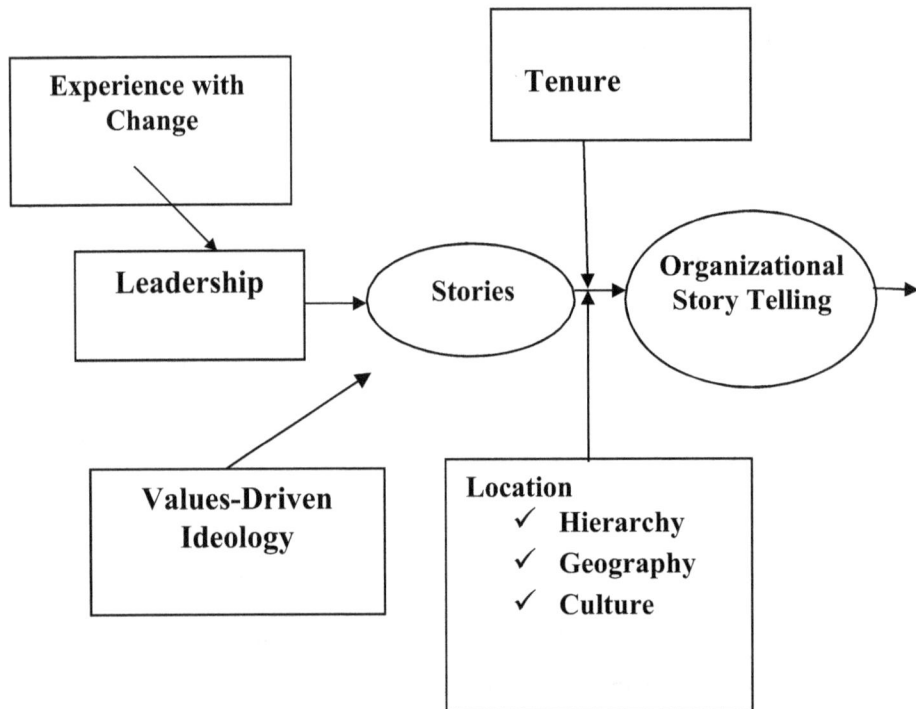

*Figure 1.* Laying the foundation: A conceptual framework.

The Art of Storytelling

# Storytelling

*Knowledge, then, is experiences and stories,*
*and intelligence is the apt use of experience*
*and the creation and telling of stories.*
*(Schank, 1990)*

This chapter builds the theoretical framework upon which the dissertation lies.

The relevant contemporary leadership, organizational identity, commitment and resilience, and organizational storytelling literature are discussed and integrated within the context of turbulent economic forces. The ways in which meanings and values are conveyed under these conditions, particularly through stories within organizations, are presented and articulated as key conceptual linkages for this research. The research setting is then described, offering a prime vantage point for this phenomenon. Finally, the research questions and initial propositions guiding this study are detailed.

Starting at the beginning, why do people tell stories? This is a complex question that has challenged scholars across many domains. It has drawn a great deal of interest in the field of management and organization studies. In all areas, research consistently concludes that the narrative form, particularly in stories,

Dr. Radisha Brown

is thickly embedded with meaning.

How stories are told, the consistency and repetition of telling certain stories, the pattern of the language chosen, or even choices made to leave parts out, are all meaningful, both figuratively and literally. People construct meaning about their lives through the stories they tell (Ramer, 1997).

The challenge, of course, is for the teller and the listener to make sense out of the story being told. According to Schank (1990), people can be seen as "repositories of stories" (p. 30) and intelligence is a function of our ability to create and translate stories, where, simply, "We know what we tell, and we tell what we know" (p. 17).

The current research was originally motivated by the concept of organizational metaphors as a way to convey meaning (Morgan, 1997, 1993), drawing from the organizational symbolism literature, and has ultimately been broadened to incorporate storytelling as a medium to *generate* as well as transfer meaning. Specifically, researchers have determined that storytelling plays a complex role in translating and passing on meaning (Boje, 1991, 1995; McCollom, 1991a), particularly for leaders (Gardner & Laskin, 1995; Tichy & Cardwell, 2002).

Telling stories is a vital part of the construction of meaning and understanding in social situations (Weick, 1995). There are distinct differences between various types of narrative discourse, such as stories, sagas, and myths (Boje, 1991, 1995; McCollom, 1991a, b, c). Storytelling will be employed here in a more generic sense, further defined by storytelling in organizations about organizational events - or organizational storytelling.

The Art of Storytelling

This dissertation focused on the role of organizational storytelling during periods of upheaval, turbulence, or significant change within the organization. During these times, and retrospectively after the tremors have passed, stories convey a broad array of meaning, often serving to unify members of the organization.

In some cases, stories are believed to quell anxiety and enhance the organization's ability to navigate through difficulty (Boje, 1991; Neuhauser, 1993). Stories told by or about leaders in organizations often spread quickly and widely across organizational levels and locations. In these instances, stories can act as a stabilizing influence, and the process of telling stories itself may have a calming effect during such difficult times, providing organizational direction and focus in helping to forge a stronger sense of organizational identity and commitment (Neuhauser, 1993).

Conversely, such stories can also have a destabilizing effect, as part of a change agent's organizational transformation process or as a destructive force within the organizational culture, intended or otherwise. Even more broadly, Gardner and Laskin (1995) defined effective leaders as those who help craft identity, arguing that "a key - perhaps *the* key to leadership, as well as the garnering of a following, is the effective communication of a story" (p. 62).

This dissertation connects with and builds from the contemporary leadership literature, where leaders are increasingly defined as "managers of meaning" and organizational values serve to unite members and provides perspective to understand the degree of organizational unity displayed in stories being told (Collins & Porras, 1994; Kouzes & Posner, 1995; Collins, 2001).

Dr. Radisha Brown

Taking the profundity or "quality" of authoritative stories as far as the degree to which hierarchical parts are working together with one another and with hierarchical pioneers (worth compatibility) and versatile limit (the capacity of parts of the association to adequately react to changing business conditions or business sector strengths) crosswise over authoritative levels will culminate in a full understanding of how importance is overseen and how values are taught. These are discriminating hierarchical skills to cultivate in an environment poised for hierarchical adjustment and changes that are so essential and omnipresent today.

# Organizational Values as Glue

Values in associations are the persevering arrangement of convictions that guide behavior and conduct (Kalliath et al., 1999). They serve as a typical edge of reference (Paine, 1994) and wellspring of strength and trust (Anderson, 1997), as the manifestation of authoritative "paste," an epoxy to hold an association together throughout times of instability and change (Collins, 2001; Collins & Porras, 1996). By their extreme nature, nonetheless, values are remarkably unpredictable and can be exceptionally hard to portray or measure.

Gardner and Laskin (1995) argued that individuals inevitably hunger for an expression or articulation of worth - a point of view that one considers being genuine, excellent, and great. But they especially hunger for it in times of emergency or calamitous change, when people want a bigger informative system.

The Art of Storytelling

In numerous associations, qualities considered to be critical by senior administrators are frequently condensed and formally announced in corporate quality articulations. These quality proclamations, notwithstanding, have generally shifting degrees of legitimacy or authenticity, contingent on the degree to which hierarchical pioneers and parts are based on the underlying precepts and qualities, especially concerning how parts follow up on these qualities in actuality.

Numerous contemporary associations have profound hierarchical quality frameworks that serve to establish effective authoritative development, adjustment, and change (LeBow & Simon, 1997; O'Toole, 1995). A few components of these 'worth frameworks' are open and broadly known; others are implicit and profoundly embedded in the social fabric of the association (Senge, 1990). Pioneers all through the association should in some way or another access both measurements, and authoritative parts frequently show their attention to these 'worth frameworks' in the stories they tell.

The most vivid examples of value systems in action are frequently seen after major organizational events, such as crises, mergers, or acquisitions; then the time frame associated with widespread cultural change and the stated need to adopt a uniform organizational set of philosophies are accelerated and heightened (Mirvis & Marks, 1992).

Because of the major change event, the organization is "shocked" or destabilized. Its members often search for direction and a means to move forward. The organization's stated value systems, if

Dr. Radisha Brown

well-conceived and widely supported across the organization, serve to unite the organization in re-stabilizing and establishing a new strategic course correction.

Conversely, the absence of such values or a weak value foundation, where values are unclear or inconsistent, will directly impede the organization's ability to adapt during major periods of upheaval. In such situations, leaders must strive to ensure that conflict resolution is somehow in concert and in line with the company's core values. Clear, consistent values are vitally important given today's turbulent climate, but are also much more complex and difficult to understand.

# Organizational Identity and Commitment

This section explores the nature of identity and commitment in organizations today, further emphasizing the necessity of adaptation due to the changing nature of organizational membership in combination with dynamic market forces. The longstanding definition of organizational identity is central, distinct, and enduring for the organization and its members. Likewise, hierarchical commitment reflects the relative quality of employees' mentality toward relating to, and being included in, their associations.

Authoritative commitment is described here by acknowledgment of hierarchical objectives and qualities, eagerness to push additional exertion, and yearning to keep up enrollment in the association (Mowday et al., 1979).

The Art of Storytelling

Research shows that firms that display a clearer understanding of their organizational identity, i.e., that collectively and consistently answer "Who are we?" or, more telling, "Who do we want to be?", may possess a significant competitive advantage in harnessing the creative efforts of the diverse workforce in the face of complex market challenges (Barney, 1991; Eccles et al., 1992; Fiol, 1991; 1994; Nkomo & Cox, 1996; Pratt & Foreman, 2000).

More recent research shows that commitment to the association impacts execution positively, particularly where execution goals are clear and upheld by hierarchical prize frameworks (Siders et al., 2001). In view of the changing career contract in organizations (Rousseau, 1995; Hall & Mirvis, 1996; Hall & Moss, 1998; McCarthy & Hall, 2000), it is not clear how these dynamics come together.

Certainly, loyalties today have shifted between individuals and organizations versus the relationships in the past. Faithfulness inside associations now is regularly formed basically by assignment or mission and determined by imparted reason; such reason-driven devotion empowers flexibility in distinguishing continuous, and frequently capricious, hierarchical change (Heckscher, 1995; McCarthy & Hall, 2000).

Individuals must be increasingly resilient, life-long learners who are open to change themselves, relying on their skills and values to construct a role with which they can identify, rather than traditional identification with the organization where one is employed (Pulley, 1997). In this way, acknowledging the impact of continuous organizational change, current research increasingly

Dr. Radisha Brown

challenges the notion of an "enduring" aspect of identity that individuals possess toward organizations of which they are members, instead of posing a fluid or "adaptive" construct of organizational identity (Gioia et al., 2000).

Despite shifting organizational realities, however, a clear sense of organizational identity remains essential today, still serving as "a rudder for navigating difficult waters" (Albert et al., 2000, p. 13). Similarly, Meyer and Allen (1997) acknowledge that the forces that drive organizational commitment are changing, but point out that the study of commitment and its antecedents also remains relevant for three primary reasons:

- Organizations are de-layering, but still need a core of committed, adaptive employees

- Organizations must develop commitments with other organizations with whom they contract

- People will continue to be "naturally" committed to organizations or other endeavors, even if different than in the past

Clearly, the dynamics of organizational commitment are changing along with the ways in which identity is forged in modem organizations. Rousseau (1998, p. 219) outlined a central tenet as: "Changes, in the nature of contemporary employment, create a challenge to processes of identification by affecting the content of psychological contracts and frequently eroding existing contracts. Nonetheless, mechanisms for fostering identification endure, even if they are not always recognized." So, identity and commitment today are more continuous and *require* the capacity to change and adapt.

The Art of Storytelling

This dissertation accordingly links with contemporary identity and commitment research in seeking to better understand how commitment is built within contemporary organizations, particularly during times of change and considering the changing nature of work roles and evolving organizational relationships. One particularly cogent aspect of this linkage is organizational storytelling, as a way to rapidly bring diverse organizational members together and build organizational commitment, as detailed later in this research.

# Resilience

An important outcome of this research is a clearer understanding of the relationship between storytelling and resiliency in organizations, especially whether there is evidence that storytelling serves as an antecedent to resilience, or is associated with increased levels of resilience, in organizational members. This study views resilience as the ability of organizational members to withstand stress and volatility, working together toward common goals while facing continued uncertainty, versus crumbling under the weight of change and uncertainty.

This research proposes that storytelling, where organizational values are expressed in members' stories, serves to unify and fortify participants, building organizational commitment and strengthening resiliency. The concept of resilience (from the Latin *resilere*, to leap back or spring back) may be best conceptualized as buoyancy or the capacity to bounce back into shape after being

Dr. Radisha Brown

stretched by some force or event. As summarized in Carson et al. (2001, p. 3), "Characterized by a commonly recognized set of personal qualities, resilient individuals are alleged to resist intellectual, physical, and emotional drain in stressful situations because they are positive, focused, flexible, organized, and proactive."

On a personal level, Pulley (1997, p. 176) describes resilience as "acquiring skills and strengths so that we can move through periods of chaos and reintegration throughout our lives." Resilience is a characteristic acknowledged as increasingly important in today's fast-paced society and, more specifically, very desirable in organizations facing heightened change, where unpredictability is more prevalent, and adaptability is more necessary (Doe, 1994; Conner, 1998; Wanberg & Banas, 2000).

According to Hall (1994), in view of turbulent environmental changes, individuals and organizations must possess '3F' qualities: Fast, Flexible, and Facile (i.e., smart and quick) to be able to adapt to the changing world around them. This is in concert with the concept of protean (rapidly changing, more autonomous) careers and the need for individuals to leverage the meta-competencies of identity and adaptability to handle increased uncertainty and change (Hall & Mirvis, 1996; Hall & Moss, 1998).

Bridges (1994) views resilience as an essential characteristic for all workers in view of the increasingly project-based nature of organizational membership and defines resiliency as the ability to learn new things and "bounce back" from setbacks as well as living with uncertainty and having a sense of security from within.

The Art of Storytelling

Similarly, London (1998: 1999) suggested that people with heightened resilience possess an achievement need and confidence in their own ability for positive change, with some degree of control, are willing to take reasonable risks, need to establish why things happen to them and are willing to search for negative feedback about themselves and their interpretations of events. In this way, London (1997; 1998) espoused the broader notion of "career resilience," evidenced where people display the ability to adapt, even when facing discouraging circumstances to successfully navigate organizational change (London, 1983, 1985; London & Mone, 1987; Fine, 1991).

With long-standing roots in the study of childhood and personal development in psychology, anthropology, and sociology, recent research on resilience has focused on organizational settings, the relationship between organizational members and resilience, and evidence of common characteristics and antecedents (Hoopes, 1999; Home & Orr, 1998; Doe, 1994). Carson et al. (2001) summarized the characteristics that are typically attributed to resilient individuals through their cross-disciplinary literature review.

# Storytelling and Leading Change

Central to this dissertation is the view that organizational storytelling is a way to rapidly pass on values and meaning in complex settings. The premise explored here is that the value systems and beliefs held by members are embedded in stories and serve to guide behavior and action, facilitating resiliency and adaptive behavior.

Dr. Radisha Brown

Storytelling and leading change are interwoven, as leadership messages are passed on to organizational members in many ways, often very powerfully within the stories that move through the organization.

More broadly, stories are a particular narrative form, relatively short in duration, describing a specific event in some detail, with a fairly concrete beginning and end (McCollom, 1991b). Not all stories, however, are memorable or distinct, as the most compelling stories contain a clear central plot, interesting characters, and action, are appropriately timed (i.e. relatively short), and are told fluently (Neuhauser, 1993). "Good" stories define "relationships, a sequence of events, cause and effect, and a priority among items - *and those elements are likely to be remembered as a complex whole*" (Shaw et al., 1998, p. 42).

According to Schank (1990), the human memory is story-based, with stories being derived from many different types of sources, including culturally common stories, those heard from others, and those we craft ourselves.

Regardless of the source and format of our stories, it is a central premise to this dissertation that the ability to access, deliver, and digest stories contributes integrally to our understanding of the world around us. The following sections describe the nature of organizational storytelling to provide a broader perspective of the literature contributing directly to this research.

The Art of Storytelling

# Functions of Organizational Stories

Many researchers have studied stories as a way to convey meaning and to pass on values (Brown, 1990; Boje, 1991; 1996; Weick, 1995; Gersick et al., 2000). Storytelling is particularly powerful in organizational settings, where "stories act as a vehicle through which members can offer definitions and explanations of their work life" (Brown & Kreps, 1993, p. 49). The telling process of stories can serve to generate belief by constraining or broadening what members experience and feel.

Stories present theoretical limits for parts to thoroughly consider and comprehend occasions that have happened (Brown & Kreps, 1993; Weick, 1995), controlling thought as well as conduct. Gersick et al. (2000) contemplated stories to inspect work environment connections, referring to Louis and Sutton's (1991) confining and expressing that, through contemplating narrating, "learning that is ordinarily shrouded comes into perspective" (p. 1030).

Broadly, the purpose of stories in organizations is primarily two-fold (Neuhauser, 1993): *Grounding* to clarify key values and *Instruction* to demonstrate how things are done in a setting. Furthermore, stories function to facilitate understanding, as we remember better in the narrative. Intentions and motivation are clearer in stories, and stories can contain and express important lessons that are relevant or transferable across multiple domains (Down & King, 1999).

Storytelling is often employed in organizations to help

Dr. Radisha Brown

explain crises or great organizational challenges (Neuhauser, 1993), exemplifying the power of stories in the collective sense-making process. The collection of stories told over time is often considered a "repository of organizational intelligence," as members accumulate an understanding of how events and situations were dealt with in the past (Brown & Kreps, 1993; Kreps, 1990).

Telling a story, or hearing and reflecting upon a story, may in this vein greatly assist in the information gathering aspect of preparing for a new situation, particularly in other situations of conflict or uncertainty. As Neuhauser summarizes (1993, p. 33), "The key to the art of storytelling is the capacity to trigger dramatic and memorable pictures in the minds of the listeners."

This links with Gardner and Laskin's (1995) cognitive-based premise that leaders employ stories to change mental representation to bring about behavioral changes in others, especially when accompanied by "embodying" consonant values from the stories in the leader's own action.

## Alternate Perspectives on Stories

Not all perspectives of organizational storytelling or storytelling-based research are straightforward or clear-cut. Many postmodern and critical viewpoints (e.g., Boje, 1995; 1999; Boyce, 1996) challenge the notion that a story can be explained or analyzed in any individual way; instead, multiple voices and multiple realities must be considered, given the vast array of interpretations endemic to a social constructivist ideology. Boje et al. (1999) specifically cautioned about the hegemonic aspects of the storytelling research process, as narrators, by definition, privilege particular "fragments" of stories.

Similarly, Boyce (1996) described the "emergent challenges" inherent in research on stories; in particular, that researchers "examine the perspective with which they undertake story and storytelling work in organizations" (p. 21) to more fully appreciate - and acknowledge - the underlying dynamics of power, individual bias (including, and especially, the researcher), and the impact of the prevailing culture to skew interpretation. Researching stories in organizations must be carefully undertaken to appropriately represent as many of the "voices" as possible.

Consequently, it is important to fully recognize that all researchers, like all storytellers, carry a personal bias in the ways in which *they* make sense out of the stories they hear or tell, themselves. Being aware of this bias and presenting data as carefully and openly as possible are essential elements of storytelling-based research.

It is hereby acknowledged that the stories assembled and presented in this research were studied in a structured, methodologically consistent manner, but they nonetheless represented and, consequently privileged by me, the act of telling the story of this research process.

## Organizational Storytelling in Use

Researchers and practitioners have become increasingly

Dr. Radisha Brown

aware of the power of organizational stories as "potent carriers of values and memory" (Stewart, 1998, p. 165). Many notable corporations, including IBM, Xerox, Federal Express, 3M, Berkshire Hathaway, Red Robin International, Hallmark, and Eastman Chemical, explicitly use storytelling in their executive communication processes to convey organizational values, impart lessons, and explain complex tasks (Anfuso, 1998; Stewart, 1998; Wylie, 1998; Shaw et al., 1998).

Prominent business leaders at GE, Barnes & Noble, Mattel, Hewlett- Packard, and McDonald's overtly recognize the importance of using stories in their leadership practices to deliver complex messages, particularly "in an increasingly technological and impersonal world" (Dennehy, 1999, p. 40).

Storytelling itself also helps leaders seem more flexible, approachable, less threatening, and more confident (Wylie, 1998). Consequently, management training and development professionals have acknowledged the power of storytelling to impart culture and values, and are implementing storytelling skill-building, through coaching and facilitated practice, to managers at all levels to build their leadership storytelling expertise (Kaye & Jacobson, 1999; Breuer, 1999; Berman & Oleck, 1998; Hildebrand, 1998).

Hyperbole aside, as reported on the opening line of a Fortune article on leadership (Stewart, 1998, p. 165), "Nothing serves a leader better than a knack for narrative." The research here, however, is not necessarily intended to help leaders or managers in organizations to be able to tell stories better, or even to tell better stories. Instead, this dissertation strives to explain and emphasize how essential The Art of Storytelling "everyday stories" are as an indicator of organizational life and vitality, stressing the critical role leaders at all organizational levels play in cultivating this medium.

# Storytelling and Identity

Stories and storytelling can serve to strengthen organizational identity and cast a positive vision of the company. Neuhauser (1993) described many types of such positive stories often found in organizations, all of which contribute toward engaging and enhancing a sense of organizational identity; one could also readily envision the potential for the opposite impact, where negative stories foster contrary attitudes toward the protagonists.

This dissertation explored the function of stories as a channel or conceptual pathway to establish common values, strengthen identity and build commitment as a unifying, bonding framework for organizational members to respond to difficult situations, change, and turbulence, in line with similar research by Brown (1990). As summarized in Brown and Kreps (1993, p.49), "Of course, stories have meaning. But stories also persuade, reinforce, define, and educate (Dennehy, 1999). Further, stories grow from and present different organizational value sets, steering members and decision makers toward a view of the organization (Kreps, 1983). In sum, organizational storytelling is a compelling activity that pervades all aspects of organizational life.

Stories help to form organizational value systems, which the storytelling process reinforces on an ongoing basis across the

Dr. Radisha Brown

organization. Storytelling is tightly intertwined with leadership, organizational values, and organizational commitment, especially during times of turbulence and change, where resilience is so important. Interpreting stories and analyzing patterns in storytelling will provide insight to improve our understanding of organizational change processes and to make more sense out of organizational behavior during periods of turmoil.

# SECTION

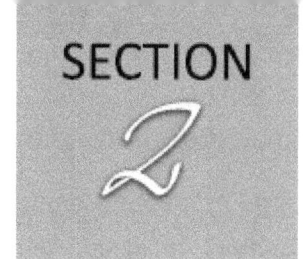

# REVIEW OF THE LITERATURE

This literature review consists of two main sections and a summary. Following an introduction, the first section discusses the current literature on organizational change and change strategies, with an interim summary. The second section discusses the role of storytelling in leading change and as a strategy for change. The chapter ends with a summary.

Change is a constant. It is a thread woven into our professional and personal lives. The process of change occurs in all aspect of our lives. It can take place in the physical environment that surrounds us. It occurs in international and national events, in the organizational structure, in socioeconomic and political issues and their remedies and in social and cultural norms and values.

In the context of business or organization, change is referred to the speed with which the industry and trade launches new and innovative services or products on a regular basis (Jones, 2004). Given that the world is becoming more multifaceted as well as increasingly unified, changes apparently do not affect people much. Therefore, changes more often take place randomly and frequently.

This demands that organizations improve their capabilities to effectively meet and manage the changes, which in turn enhances their level of competency. The world in which we live is subjected to

Dr. Radisha Brown

continuous change. Changes have been and are being made regularly.

In the year 2006, Fleming and Senior depicted a prospective future and the ways it will influence people and their enthusiasm to accept changes (Jones, 2004). The future organizations will be comprised of fewer management layers that will, in turn, incorporate fewer employees working together. However, a reduction in the number of employees will result in greater pressure that will force employees to work harder and for longer times.

Fleming and Senior also assumed that there might be potential changes in the working pattern of a workplace (Jones, 2004). For any specific organization, there will be more than one workplace and a larger population of employees will be expected to continue their duties from home. The characteristics of employees will also change since the birth rate in the future is expected to decrease and consequently the population of older people will rise.

As a result, the number of average-aged people in an organization will increase (Jones, 2010). The characteristics of employees' skill are also expected to alter in the future. This change will demand that employees become more skilled. The rise in demand for new skills will be certainly due to continuous advancement in technologies and competency level.

According to both the researchers, due to expected changes in the future, employees will get more job opportunities and the self-employment rate will also increase. Since most of the future employees will be of average age, improvements in pension schemes will be necessary (Senior & Fleming, 2006).

The Art of Storytelling

At present, the majority of organizations across the globe function under escalating demands for change. Due to high competition, the market has drastically changed with respect to technological advancement, increased customer demands, and globalization (Harenstam et al., 2004). This rapidity of change requires organizations to change their organizational behavior and policies so that they can respond effectively to market shifts (Nonas, 2005).

On the other hand, Beer and Nohria (2000) argued that high paced changes in development programs and projects usually result in disappointing results. For any organization to effectively manage change, competency must increase.

Change competency is defined as the capability of an organization to effectively manage the changes in the environment and to be competent enough to become the part of this continuous process. Change competence is also referred to as the selection of an appropriate change strategy in line with the company goals and experience of employees regarding the change process (Beer & Nohria, 2000).

Societal changes, political trends, consumer buying habits, economic climates, management policy or structure, employment levels and financial resources all affect an organization's ability to change (Buckner & Wakefield, 2006). However, change is dynamic, constant and alarming for some organizations. Despite the expectations that leadership has for their organization, the organization's ability to reach those goals often depends on how well the organization responds to change (Buckner & Wakefield, 2006).

Dr. Radisha Brown

According to Buckner and Wakefield, the leadership management of an organization plays a significant role in managing turbulent environments at the time of the change process. The fundamental responsibility of leadership management is to convey the goals and vision in accord with the impending change. Buckner and Wakefield (2006) argued that employees can generally work harder due to increases in pressure, but to enhance the effectiveness of their work, it is imperative to clearly communicate why they are required to do so and the aims and objectives behind it.

Moreover, Buckner and Wakefield also specified that it is crucial that the person in charge carry through with the change and remain patient, because positive outcomes do not come at once. In recent times, there has been a significant increase in the interest of leadership management regarding the influence of culture on the ability to learn and change. Understanding planned and development change or organizational learning is not possible without taking culture into consideration as a fundamental source of resistance to change (Volkoff & Strong, 2013).

Culture has a huge impact on the process of change; culture will win the race against strategy every time. This is due to the fact that a modified strategy will not result in the required change unless the effective changes in culture are also being made accordingly. The leadership management cannot simply execute organizational changes by means of systems and structures only. They need to focus on their current organizational culture and determine whether their existing culture is adaptive to change; if not, they need to establish a new and stronger basis of unity (Hirschhorn, 2000). It is important for

The Art of Storytelling

organizations to be aware of their organizational culture, holistic nature and the way in which their employees affect each other.

The rapid rise in the change has forced organizations and their employees to focus on the bigger side of the picture and gain awareness of how changes in events and business policies can affect them. At present, the dynamic business environment and technological advancement demand great changes be made in the operations of the organization and its respective organizational structure (Volkoff & Strong, 2013). It is noteworthy that, today, change is prevalent and has turned out to be an essential element in maintaining the competitive edge of an organization (Abrahamson, 2000). Therefore, the old bureaucratic management style is now incompetent to meet the challenges of a changing business environment.

To effectively meet the changes, it is imperative for organizations to strengthen their workforce so that change does not unduly affect their profitability. The prospects of an organization greatly depend upon the success of change projects and consequently, immense endeavors are required for successful implementation of these projects. Simpler processes, increased productivity, shorter delivery durations and increased employee welfare are some of the typical examples of the objectives of organizational changes (Jarvenpaa & Eloranta, 2000).

According to a 1991 survey of major electronic companies in the United States, just 38% of those engaged in total quality programs reported that through the program, more than 10% of their quality defects were improved. The results of the survey illustrated that

Dr. Radisha Brown

nearly 50-70% of reengineering endeavors do not achieve their targets.

# Organizational Change and Change Strategies

The term *organizational change* refers to the process by which an organization optimizes its performance as it targets and acquires an ideal position in the market (Jones, 2004). From a subjective point of view, organizational change takes place as a response to turbulent business environments or in reaction to a crisis. Moreover, a more pro-active perspective of organizational change is change prompted by senior management. This organizational change is particularly evident in organizations that experience a shift in senior management (Haveman et al., 2001).

The main causes of organizational change can be determined in the light of the following theories: dialectical theory, life-cycle theory, and teleological theory. According to the teleological viewpoint, organizational change is an effort to attain an ideal state in the market through a continuous process of planning, execution, assessment, and reformation. The life-cycle theory argues that an organization is a body whose functions typically depend upon the external environment involving various cycles in the phases of birth, growth, maturation, and declination. The dialectical theory assumes that an organization is, to a certain extent, similar to a multicultural society with contrasting principals (Volkoff & Strong, 2013).

In the context of this theory, organizational change is evident when one force dominates over others. As a result, the rest of the companies in the market tend to establish new organizational goals and values to remain competitive in the market. Change denotes a new state of affairs that is distinctive from the existing state of affairs. Therefore, organizational change signifies that a new state of business in an organization is distinctive from the previous one (Salminen, 2000).

Several different sources stimulate the need for change. These sources might be internal as well as external. The external driving forces behind change include competitors, customers, technology, and regulators. The internal drivers to change include outdated products and services, fresh market opportunities, increasing diversity in the workforce and new strategic directions. The decision of an organization to strive for change either depends upon the failures of its projects and business operations or on new business opportunities in the market (Oreg et al., 2011). Change in an organization can also be motivated by an exterior change agent, which takes the initial step towards the endeavor of change.

The majority of organizations incorporate change in their business structure or operations due to external pressures rather than internal aspirations. According to Oreg and colleagues (2011), change is stimulated by an awareness or experience of potential threat or loss, or due to new opportunities.

In sum, organizational change is required in circumstances when the present performance of an organization or its operational

The Art of Storytelling

business strategies are no longer equivalent with the internal requirements of the company or with the exterior business environment and competency level.

With respect to developing organizations, two different notions are generally notable, operational change and organizational change. Yet, practically both concepts robustly intertwine with each other and are hard to separate because changes in one unit of systems influence other units (Salminen, 2000). Therefore, each attempt at a successful change must involve both operational and organization elements and characteristics.

According to scholars, organizational change can be achieved by changing three different levels of an organization. First is changing employees, which means that changes must be made in their behavior, attitudes, values, and skills. Second is changing the procedures and systems that encompass reporting relationships, rewarding systems and work design (Dahl, 2011). The third and last is changing the overall climate or culture of an organization.

A change initiated by a project can be either cultural. i.e., modifications in the structure processes, systems, attitudes, values, and skills, or technical, i.e., advancement in the technology or physical environment. Salminen (2000) put forth that the artificial separation of the two types of changes typically takes place due to boundaries between different research traditions and academic limitations.

Social researchers view organizational changes from an individual's perspective whereas operational changes are viewed from the perspective of operations research and industrial engineering (Salminen 2000). Moreover, the subject matter and the extent of the change, its meticulousness and necessity might also differentiate the types of efforts required for the two changes.

Frequently, large-scale changes in an organizational strategy and culture are often classified as evolutionary changes, incremental changes, fixing issues, fine-tuning and making necessary adjustments and modifications in the procedures (Dahl, 2011). The changes should be made in such a manner that the implementation of the change only enhances the performance of an organization and does not change the organization.

Elementary changes are as well known as fundamental or innovative change, turnaround, renovation, reorientation or refocus (Buhanist, 2000). A change can be either premeditated (planned) or accidental (unplanned). The process of change can be either slow or fast. It may affect many business units of an organization or only a few. The number of components of an organization depends on the degree of change that is being implemented.

Change can occur in all aspects of business from the broadest, most conceptual level (for example, changing the overall business culture of an organization) to the narrowest and most confined (for example, replacing outdated instruments with new advanced ones). Nevertheless, change can take place around two basic spheres: change in operational strategy or pertaining to the organization (Griffin & Moorhead, 2011).

Although a majority of scholars believe that the topic of organizational change is currently the center of attraction for most
The Art of Storytelling

organizations, a difference of opinion exists regarding its implementation and management. Even though the opinions of a few scholars contradict each other, they still must be viewed as harmonizing with one another (Griffin & Moorhead, 2011).

Every approach related to organizational change is distinctive, but still provides a partial perspective about it. By synchronizing insight from each approach, however, a comprehensive understanding of organizational change can be established. In fact, this coordinated insight of organizational change is expected to be richer and more effective as compared to the adaption of a single approach (Poole & Van de Ven, 2005).

Dr. Radisha Brown

The Art of Storytelling

# Organizational Development

Organizational change is frequently handled under organizational development. Organizational development is a field of study that originates from and is based on the behavioral science disciplines (anthropology, system theory, sociology, organization theory, management and psychology). The role of organizational development is to address change and to determine the impacts of change on the organization and its employees. Therefore, effectual organizational development facilitates the organization and its employees in managing change in a more effective manner (Smissen et al., 2013).

To introduce a planned change in an organization, various strategies can be designed so that efforts are made to establish a cohesive team that works together to enhance organizational functioning. Even though change is specified, there are numerous approaches to cope with it effectively; however, some of them are effective while others are not. Organizational development helps an organization cope with changing business environments, both externally and internally. It generally does so by initiating endeavors for a planned change.

In the field of business, organizational development is a comparatively fresh approach for organizations. On the other hand,

Dr. Radisha Brown

the approach regarding the professional development of employees has been acknowledged and implemented in a majority of organizations in the past. Nonetheless, some vagueness still exists regarding the approach of organizational development (Smissen et al., 2013). The chief principles of organizational development and professional development are similar, but a crucial divergence exists in focus.

The aim of organizational development is to enhance the overall profitability, responsiveness to a turbulent environment, and productivity of an organization. The aim of professional development is to improve employee's capabilities and effectiveness. Their targets are achieved by involving several processes that are designed to deal with specific issues. The endeavors of organizational development, whether facilitated by an external professional or by an internal expert, are a consistent result in a planned change inside the teams and organization (Smissen et al., 2013).

Change in an organization is not triggered until its requirement becomes crucial for the survival of an organization, usually because both organizations and employees oppose change. In general, organizations and employees do not embrace change until they are forced to do so.

Thomas and Hardy (2011) argued that pain triggers change in an organization. Pain arises when employees or organizations pay the cost of missing a golden opportunity or enter a perilous state (Thomas & Hardy, 2011). In such circumstances, change is required to eliminate the pain. According to this perception, change will not be appreciated because it is a good idea. It will take place because
The Art of Storytelling

the loss or pain suffered by an organization and its employees is sufficient enough to compel implementing the change.

Thus, the person in charge should emphasize the absolute need for incorporating change within an organization, instead of just focusing on its benefits (Thomas & Hardy, 2011). It is important for the person in charge of the change to acknowledge this approach and make others realize that there is no other option for a struggling organization.

# Targets of Organizational Change

Extensive factors influence organizational change. These factors are mainly related to changes in the external environment and strategies that will facilitate in enhancing the internal administrative efficacy. Prior to planning for change, organizations must focus on the potential reasons for change. These reasons generally encompass the internal situation of an organization in conjunction with the external environment (Erwin & Garman, 2010).

Recognizing the key reasons behind the change assists the change agents to identify the factors that must be changed. The most potential targets of organizational change take account of present strategy, organizational culture, vision, the structure of an organization, its style of leadership, systems and production technology (Yang et al., 2009).

The vision of an organization mainly comprises organizational core values and includes values that are adopted in accordance with pressures from the external environment. It is imperative to determine the core values of an organization during the process of organizational change so that they can be preserved. The strategy of a company typically represents its long-standing goals along with the steps and resources required to accomplish them.

A company can divide its chief strategy into overall strategic change (e.g., multiple angle management), enterprise strategy change (e.g., low-cost strategy), or global expansion strategy change (Yang, et al., 2009). The culture of an organization typically represents the norms and values of its employees, their behavior towards work and their perceptions.

It is easier to manage explicit culture as compared to implicit culture. The structure of an organization refers to the authority relations and official system of duty of an organization. Changes made in the structure of an organization result in a transformed horizontal differentiation, level of formalization, vertical disintegration and power allocation. Production technology includes knowledge, technology, capabilities, and resources such as tools, equipment, and computers that are required for transforming inputs into outputs (Erwin & Garman, 2010). The 'system' comprises formal policies, regulations, and procedures (such as methods for assessing performance, goal budget system and reward system), which are required for operating the organization.

Leadership refers to an influential force within an organization. The style of leadership typically influences the interface of its employees and group dynamics. The targets of organizational change will certainly influence each other (Erwin & Garman, 2010). For instance, the actualization of the vision of an organization relies

The Art of Storytelling

on its strategies and culture. Hence, in the process of organizational change, the vision of the company should be considered so that different change targets can be considered to successfully accomplish the organizational change.

# Planning for Organizational Change

Prior to initiating an organizational change, it is imperative for the senior management of an organization to design strategies and forecast prospective issues. Various researchers and practitioners have proposed a technique known as force-field analysis that can be used by organizations to plan and manage organizational change (Erwin & Garman, 2010).

This analysis technique is relatively simple and effective. It assumes that organizational behavior is a consequence of stability between the two disparate forces. Change might only be triggered if there is a shift in balance among these two forces. The driving force is a force that influences a positive and enhanced change. Driving forces of an organizational change can be the customers or clients, changing business trends and resources.

Resisting an organizational change are restrictive forces, which are characterized as barriers to preferred change. While both opposing forces are active in an organization, a state of balance exists within an organization (Erwin & Garman, 2010).

This balance implies that, when the weights of restrictive forces and driving forces are comparatively the same, an organization will stay static. As new changes become effective in an organization, a new state of balance will be established as a result the organization will return to "quasi-stationary equilibrium" (Griffin & Moorhead, 2011).

Force-field analysis assists an organization in designing two major strategies. One strategy is used by the employees to determine their current organizational framework, brainstorming and forecasting the potential changes that are currently taking place in the business environment. The other strategy acts as a tool for executing the change. In the former, the force-field analysis becomes a technique that can be utilized by the organizations in environmental scanning, which is, in turn, beneficial for strategic planning and through which an organization can maintain a record of potential and impending changes (Griffin & Moorhead, 2011). These changes range from social and cultural trends to employee turnover or replacement of outdated equipment.

Anticipating an organizational change prior to its implementation helps organizations effectively prepare to confront its consequences. Force-field analysis also plays a significant role in examining the potential resources that can withstand organizational change and any anticipating restrictive forces. This pre-planning and analysis facilitates the design of strategies to effectively implement change within an organization.

# The process of Organizational Change

Force-field analysis is an initial step of organizational change. There are many other methods for processing an organizational change. Egan (2010) proposed a simple and straightforward process to bring about an organizational change.

His proposed process has three steps:

- A critical evaluation of the present state of an organization

- The creation of the desired organizational state

- Designing an effective strategy that shifts the system from present to desired organizational state

Undoubtedly, Lewin's theory (2006) influenced Egan, given that both essentially emphasize evaluation and planning (Brusoni & Rosenkranz, 2014). Additionally, Egan (2010) claimed that planning must be directed to an action that generates positive and beneficial results that, in turn, enhance the overall performance of an organization. Therefore, planning as well as organizational change should be intended to accomplish a specific goal.

As the need for organizational change is recognized, an organization must follow three steps to bring about the desired change. The first step is to critically evaluate the present state of an organization. This can be done with the help of force-field analysis technique (Brusoni & Rosenkranz, 2014). This step will help the

Dr. Radisha Brown

organization identify the driving forces behind the preferred change and the restrictive forces that can act as a barrier to the desired organizational change.

The second step in the process of organizational change involves the creation of the desired organizational state. This step can be completed through sessions of brainstorming that chiefly involve the leadership management of an organization. Effective brainstorming sessions help management develop plans for the future. While the need that triggered the change is undeniable, there are numerous ways in which change can take place inside an organization.

The third and the most crucial step in the process of organizational change is designing an effective strategy that shifts the system from the present to the desired organizational state (Brusoni & Rosenkranz, 2014). The strategy is further classified into several plans that can be put into practice to overcome restrictive forces in an organization.

This is basically a political process that encourages employees to come together and make use of their collective power. Power is crucial for bringing about organizational change (Buchanan, 2013). It cannot be considered either good or bad, since it simply facilitates management in achieving their aims and objectives.

Effective organizational changes are only possible when the experts of change combine forces to bring about the preferred change within an organization by utilizing formal as well as informal networks.

The Art of Storytelling

# Strategies for Implementing Organizational Change

It is essential for the management of an organization to combine the resources and workforce when moving an organizational development endeavor from a planning phase to the implementation stage (Buchanan, 2013). There are four sets of power tools that can be acquired by the employees of an organization for gaining power essential for moving towards organizational change. These tools are as follows: Resources (which includes staff), materials, funds and time.

# Supports that Encompass Backing, Authorization, Authenticity, and Endorsement

The first strategy in executing an organizational change involves the collection of a maximum number of the above-mentioned power tools. Once this is done, the employees can plant seeds of support for the planned organizational change. This is important to convey the critical need for planned change to others (Buchanan, 2013).

The next strategy is to present the change in a manner that makes it less intimidating and hence easier to promote. For example, it is simpler to incorporate an organization change if the desired change is performed on a trial basis, is reversible if desired or outcomes have not been achieved, is executed in small steps, is appropriate with respect to current direction of an organization, is

Dr. Radisha Brown

consistent and familiar with the past organization's experience and is fabricated on the earlier projects or commitments of an organization (Brusoni & Rosenkranz, 2014).

This packaging must be accomplished before presenting the organizational development's endeavors to the person in charge of the change. However, the person responsible for creating this package will be involved for further assistance in packaging and selling of the proposed change.

Establishing alliances with other organizations having the same interest is considered an essential strategy throughout the executing phase of organizational change. Prior to implementation, support from all the different levels of that organization that are expected to be affected by the change must be gathered of organizational change. it is convenient for change masters to make use of their informal networks, instead of discussing the issues in formal meetings, to cater to concerns or questions from supporters regarding the proposed organizational change (Buchanan, 2013).

However, pre-meetings can provide a platform for addressing the concerns of supporters or employees regarding the designed organizational change (Brusoni & Rosenkranz, 2014). In addition, pre-meetings provide an opportunity for responsible employees to trade some of the power tools they have utilized to establish support.

The Art of Storytelling

# Resistance to Change

Whether minor or major, each type of change will encounter resistance. This section of the literature review discusses some causes and types of resistance to change at the organizational level.

> *Some employees resist organizational changes because they lack a vision for the future, are short on the capabilities required to effectively manage the change, or fear replacement and/or relocation.*

# Individual Resistance

Why does resistance to change occur? What are the key factors that promote resistance? Resistance to change prevails because some employees fear the change (Fugate et al., 2012). They believe that any kind of change in the structure of an organization might affect their employment, so, they resist it. Another reason is

Dr. Radisha Brown

that most of the employees are not familiar with the benefits of a change. It is the nature of individuals to accumulate habits easily and follow a certain routine. Therefore, any kind of change might disrupt their daily routine. Initially, change represents the unknown (Fugate et al., 2012).

It could mean the likelihood of disappointment, the surrendering or attenuation of one's span of power and control. On the other hand, it might be possible that the planned change does not have any effect on the performance and productivity of an organization. Hence, any of these conceivable outcomes can cause mistrust and in this manner fear, naturally bringing resistance to endeavors related to change.

Moreover, the shift from the current state to a changed state is hard for both the organization and its employees. On an individual level, it is essential to remind a person that each move or change effort starts with a finishing that is the closure of the present state.

The initial step headed for change is to revise the methodology of closure. The potential outcomes of a change must be acknowledged and managed before people can completely embrace the change (Erwin & Garman, 2010). Although the approaching change is required, a feeling of misfortune will exist because our sense of self-being is characterized by our responsibilities, roles, and context. Therefore, any kind of change compels us to redefine ourselves and our reality. This revision is not simple.

The Art of Storytelling

> *Resistance to change is defined as an enthusiasm of deceiving authorities.*

Resistance to change is assumed to be one of the most significant factors that influence the success of organizational change that encompasses new policies, the latest organizational structure, and technological advancement. More than half of the attempts of organizational change fail and resistance to change is believed to be a chief reason. In the recent times, researchers are more interested in studying behavior reaction (Erwin & Garman, 2010).

Resistance is a sort of inaction and action. Resistance to change occurs within an organization when its employees deliberately perform actions of omission and defiance. However, resistance to change can be diminished if employees exhibit acquiescent behavior.

There are certain limitations to the concept. Interests of senior management must not be privileged above the interests of employees (Erwin & Garman, 2010). Thomas et al (2011) argued that resistance to change prevails in situations where employees distrust management or have experienced disappointing change outcomes in the past.

Resistance to change is an attempt to save conventional social relationships that might be at risk because of change (Thomas et al., 2011). Some employees resist organizational changes because they lack a vision for the future, are short on the capabilities required

Dr. Radisha Brown

to effectively manage the change, or fear replacement and/or relocation.

# Organizational Resistance to Change

Resistance to change occurs at the organizational level too. However, because organizations are mainly composed of individuals, the degree to which employees can manage the change symbolizes the organizational capacity for change (Erwin & Garman, 2010). Apart from individuals' behavior, there are other factors that contribute to resistance to change. Some of these factors are listed below.

- **Inertia.** Inertia is believed to be one of the strongest forces that resist the organization and its employees to execute organization change (Erwin & Garman, 2010). Due to the burden of excess work, the necessity of implementing a change diminishes.

- **Lack of clear instruction.** If all the instructions and information regarding the implementation of organizational change are not clearly communicated with the employees, different perspectives and expectations concerning the change might prevail (Erwin & Garman, 2010).

- **Low-risk environment.** employees usually resist change in organizations where managers do not encourage change and blame employees for the

The Art of Storytelling

failure of initiatives (Thomas et al., 2011). They prefer to work in safer and low-risk environments. As a result, they do not appreciate change even though it is well-planned.

- **Lack of sufficient resources**. The lack of adequate resources is assumed to be the most significant factor that leads to organizational resistance. If an organization does not acquire adequate resources such as workforce, funds and time to effectively bring about the change, the endeavors to make the change will weaken or dissolve completely (Choi & Ruona, 2010).

All the above factors and other aspects specific to organizations can destabilize efforts to make the desired change and erode al resistance to it.

# Successful Methods for Addressing Resistance to Change

Recognizing the chief drivers of resistance to change can assist the leadership management to design effective strategies to address resistance to change. There are many reasons why employees present a negative reaction to change (Choi & Ruona, 2010). The chief reason that employees resist change is a personal loss. Most employees fear that they might lose some of the following due to organizational change.

**Security**. Employees fear the loss of their employment because of organizational change which might result in lessening of workforce or automation.

**Money.** Employees are afraid that there will be cutbacks in their salaries and other incentives. They are also concerned about potential overtime responsibilities that might be required, to effectively manage the change. Finally, they fear a rise in personal expenses if the desired change results in reallocation of employees to locations that are far from their home.

**Friends and important contacts**. A change in location because of organizational change can result in the loss of friends and important contacts. Therefore, employees resist change because they do not want to lose their contacts (Seo et al., 2012).

**Power and control**. Employees fear losing the power and control associated with their current position.

**Freedom and authority**. Organizational changes, such as structural changes, often result in the change of leadership management. Therefore, employees are concerned about their relationship with their new boss. They fear that new management or boss can replace personal freedom and confidence with close supervision, that in turn diminishes the opportunity for decision-making. Employees also worry that the new boss might withdraw their authority. As a result, they suffer the loss of authority and control over their subordinates (Seo et al., 2012).

Resistance to organizational change must not be regarded in terms of defiance and confrontations. Instead, it should be The Art of Storytelling recognized as a force or challenge that helps organizations overcoming any threats or negative aspects of change that are identified by critics (Piderit, 2000). It is the responsibility of senior management to encourage those employees who tend to distrust the planned change and challenge it.

Such employees should be talked to separately about the benefits of the planned change so that their ambiguities vanish. However, unconvinced people are assumed to be the best people to highlight the issues associated with the change and can also to fix them. Stanley et al. (2005) suggested the learning and teaching approach for dealing with the employees who resistant change. Teaching or training are the best practices to convince and earn the support of individuals to play their role in the change process.

It is crucial for the leadership management to refocus their change efforts if a large degree of resistance to change persist (Geller, 2002). The process of refocusing includes the involvement of other employees, listening and receiving feedback from them, encouraging employees and encouraging their ownership of the change process. In order to enhance the acceptance of planned change on the individual, it is necessary to break down the process and reconstruct it (Gotsill & Natchez, 2007).

In the first phase of communication, if the employees fail to comprehend the organizational change or fail to see the vision for the future, it is important to reconstruct the change process. Reconstruction allows the employees to see the big and brighter side of the picture and their responsibilities in the change process.

It is vital for change agents to take every step to widen the

Dr. Radisha Brown

sphere of employee involvement (Axelrod, 2002). The process of organizational change should be conducted in a democratic manner, despite the fact that managers at the top level of the organization possess formal authority. Instead of the conventional command-and-control approach, it is vital to creating a democratic environment in the workplace where the employees are treated with reverence and their intelligence and opinion are respected.

Integration of employees into the change process resolves the issue of lack of organizational support required for successful change because it changes the effort into an institutional process (Battilana & Casciaro, 2012). It is essential for managers to establish a relationship of trust with their employees, showing confidence and commitment of all the members of the organization. Most of the employees disagree with the statement that "take care of the organization and organization will take care of you." Perhaps in the past, the employees did not have much idea but nowadays employees are smart enough to provide logical reasons for fearing loss of employment.

Employees prefer to work in flow instead of changing their direction of work in improving the performance of the organization. Therefore, it is imperative for change masters to overcome this approach and encourage the employees to actively participate in the process of change (Battilana & Casciaro, 2012).

Once the design of the change process is approved, the leadership management should establish support from the employees (Kotter & Cohen, 2002). Lack of support and commitment will lead to a failed change implementation process.

The Art of Storytelling

It is must for every business organization to employ principals of continuous improvement and organizational learning. It is a vital approach to maintain the records of the past changes because past records can be utilized by the present organizational leaders to avoid the mistakes of the past.

Dr. Radisha Brown

The Art of Storytelling

# Different Types of Change

Organizational change can take place in different forms. Initially, the change can be characterized as invasive or non-invasive or as potential threats or opportunities. It is possible that a few changes affect the business environment only and not a group of employees, whereas most changes directly impact the group, such as the introduction of a new manager as a part of the change. The changes can be made on a large scale or vice versa.

Large-scaled changes tend to alter the overall business culture of an organization (Oreg & Sverdlik, 2011). On the other hand, small-scale changes might only influence a small number of employees.

Changes can also be characterized in terms of controllability and predictability. For instance, for a change is predictable as well as controllable, the only option for the employees is to select the appropriate time to execute the planned change. The benefit of these types of changes is that the methodology for change can be executed when the change agents are prepared and have sufficient time. In contrast to predictable and controllable changes, change can also be uncontrollable and unpredictable. Such changes are expected to present potentially immense challenges and difficulties for the

Dr. Radisha Brown

organization (Poole & Van de Ven, 2004). The organizational changes can be regarded as planned or unplanned, episodic or continuous. The following section compares the four types of change.

# Planned vs. Unplanned Change

Planned changes are usually executed by change agents who acquire complete understanding about the change and organizational structure where change is required (Oreg & Sverdlik, 2011). Planned change always tends to enhance the performance of the organization. Desired goals are defined prior to the implementation of change. In contrast to planned change, unplanned change does not always occur by the will of individuals. It usually does not steer the organization in a desirable direction. Other major differences between unplanned change and planned change lie in the extent to which the change can be scripted, controlled and choreographed.

Theories of planned change focus on the ways in which the change can be controlled or administrated, whereas theories of unplanned change argue that change is a forced initiative that cannot necessarily be effectively handled or organized (Poole & Van de Ven, 2004).

# Continuous vs. Episodic Change

Changes can also be classified, according to their cadence, as continuous or episodic. Episodic change is discontinuous, intermittent and deliberate. Continuous change is an evolving,

The Art of Storytelling

cumulative, and on-going process. Episodic change usually takes place while an organization transitions out of its current state of equilibrium. It utilizes a discrete time interval to get accomplished and it usually results in the change of technology or key personnel (Poole & Van de Ven, 2004). In contrast, continuous change encompasses cumulative, ongoing and evolving organizational changes. In general, a change can be illustrated as grounded and positioned in enduring updates of work processes. The concept of continuous change illustrates that those diminutive, consistent modifications, which are implemented simultaneously across the business units within the organization, can cumulate and bring about a significant organizational change.

The ways of executing continuous and episodic change are different. An episodic change is generally executed over a short time interval and is frequently well-designed from initial to final steps; all steps of change are clearly defined prior to the implementation of change. This type of change is normally executed by change masters (Choi, 2011). A continuous change typically involves minor modifications and enhancements in daily routine processes that can come into view immediately. While implementing continuous change, change masters must understand the ongoing changes. This understanding can be developed by means of effective communication (Nonas, 2005).

Dr. Radisha Brown

The Art of Storytelling

# Different Models of Organizational Change

# Lewin's Three-Step Model

Kurt Lewin's 1947 model of change is still functional and pertinent (Fig. 2) despite numerous revisions. One of the major points of Lewin's theory is that change is not just a single step, but it happens through various steps and levels.

More importantly, when we are concerned with the psychological stage, then change is a great journey instead of a simple single step (Burnes & Cooke, 2013). The journey of change may comprise various levels of errors, lack of understanding, etc.

A theory related to change based on three (3) stages was presented by Kurt Lewin.

**Stage 1: Unfreeze.** Unfreezing is the first step of change transition. This stage of unfreezing is very important because it helps to familiarize people with the world of change. This stage is about preparing for change (Burnes & Cooke, 2013). It includes accepting that change is essential, will enhance the current situation and helps us prepare to move away from our present safe place. This introductory stage is the process of making ourselves ready, especially if we realize the necessity and urgency of change.

**Step 2: Change (Transition).** The most important thing after unfreezing the individuals who will be involved in the change is to take the steps toward change. After unfreezing people, the most difficult thing is to make them move on to the change (Burnes & Cooke, 2013). According to Lewin's view, change is a process, not a single step. He named that process a journey or transition. This is the internal development or voyage that is made in response to a change.

This second stage happens as we create the changes that are required. Hence, this second stage is the most difficult stage because people are unsure or actively afraid of change. People should be given plenty of time to familiarize themselves with and acclimate to the proposed change. People should be given full assistance in the form of care, guidelines, and training, because at this stage support plays a vital role.

Individuals should be allowed to create their own ideas for the solution of a problem. It is also helpful to communicate the *image* of the required change, to help individuals stay on the path of change and make them comfortable.

**Step 3: Freezing or Refreezing.** This is the third stage of Lewin's model, when changes are realized and people have embraced the change, the organization is ready to refreeze. One significant measure of the success at this stage is stable a workforce (Burnes & Cooke, 2013). Establishing stability is another meaning of this stage after change happens.

The Art of Storytelling

The changes are acknowledged and turned into the new standard. People build new relationships and get comfortable with their new schedules. This can require plenty of time. Today, change can happen in a few days. There is simply no opportunity and time to get comfortable with schedules. The inflexibility of freezing does not fit with pondering change. Some change is nonstop and at times riotous, which demands incredible adaptability.

Lewin's model shows the chain of changes that a company or organization must undergo. This model provides a moderately straightforward outline that could be utilized to reshape society and is helpful in boosting performance and increasing production for organizations that confront hurdles in their development instead of working efficiently (Cummings & Worley, 2014).

The environment in which we are living is dynamic; therefore, organizations should show quicker and faster responses to change.

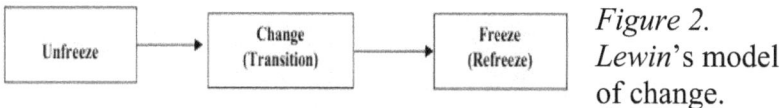

*Figure 2. Lewin*'s model of change.

# John Kotter Change Model

Kotter's Change Model provides leaders an eight- step blueprint to follow to improve an organization's ability to successfully manage transformational change (Kotter 1995). Organizations that follow Kotter's Change Model can improve their ability to successfully implement change.

Dr. Radisha Brown

# Step One: Create Urgency

The change will easily occur when every individual, department and component group of an organization is willing to make the change instead of a few people or departments of an organization. This will be helpful in creating the sense of urgency among the people who are associated with change and boosting movement toward change (Appelbaum et al., 2012). Producing the sense of urgency among the people will favor quicker change. This does not mean calling meetings to discuss competitors, glancing at poor sales statistics, or discussing poor marketing techniques, but to creating a platform and inviting related people to open talks about the current market situation and its requirements. If most of the related people favor and support the cause and need for change put before them, they are more likely to develop a sure sense of urgency.

> **Creating urgency.** Appelbaum et al. (2012) made the following suggestions for action:
>
> - Examine chances that ought to be, or could be, misused
> - Sense the alarming threats and create a picture in minds of people showing them the expected future events and problems
> - Initiate platforms of discussions and provide persuading ideas to convince people to talk and to think efficiently
> - Request backing from clients, outside shareholders and industry people to reinforce and empower your ideas.

The Art of Storytelling

# Step Two: Form a Powerful Coalition

Attracting people towards change and convincing them through persuasive ideas requires rigid leadership. This is possible only when support and full assistance is available from the leading people of the organization. You should lead, as well as manage, the process of change, because "managing" alone is insufficient (Appelbaum et al., 2012).

Seek out strong leaders among the people associated with your company or organization. To lead change, you must unite a coalition or group of persuasive people whose force and power originate from various sources, including occupational title, status, aptitude, and political support and importance.

When structured, your "change coalition" is required to act as a group, developing urgency and more energy around the necessity for change.

> **Creating coalitions.** Appelbaum et al. (2012) made the following suggestions for action:
>
> - Discover the appropriate, effective and strong leaders from your firm
> - Work on group forming inside your change coalition
> - Judge and check your group for frail zones, weaknesses and guarantee that you have a great blend of people from various sections and departments and distinctive levels inside your organization
> - Ask for a passionate response from these key people

Dr. Radisha Brown

# Step Three: Create a Vision for Change

When you start to plan for a change to happen, numerous attractive options and remedies may come to your mind. Unite these ideas into a general vision that people can understand and bear in mind effortlessly (Appelbaum et al., 2012). A vision that is crystal clear can help everybody comprehend why you're asking them to perform and accomplish the requested tasks. When people see what you're attempting to accomplish, then the guidelines and directions they're given tend to work effectively.

**Create a vision for change**. Appelbaum et al. (2012) made the following suggestions for action:

- Develop a technique to bring that vision into action
- Make sure that your change coalition can portray the vision in a few minutes
- Frequently deliver your "vision speech"
- Create a precise outline that shows your vision for your organization in future
- Evaluate the characteristics that are vital to the change

# Step Four: Communicate the Vision

Taking immediate steps after the creation of your vision increases the rate of success. You should, again and again, communicate your message instead of arranging occasional meetings. All possible efforts should be made to keep the vision fresh in the minds of people to get quick responses. By doing so, people will remember your message and speed up the process of change (Appelbaum et al., 2012).

Try to solve problems on a daily basis by using your vision. Things you do are more important and influential than what you say. Convey to people your expectations and the behavior you want, through frequent messages and demonstrations.

**Communicating the vision.** Appelbaum et al. (2012) made the following suggestions for action:

- Frequently discuss your vision of change with related people
- Freely and honestly communicate people's problems and suggestions
- Demonstrate your vision to all parts of operations - from preparation to execution. Attach everything to the vision

Dr. Radisha Brown

# Step Five: Remove Obstacles

You will get a good response from your staff and a hopeful attitude toward the process of change by following the steps above. Upon reaching this stage of the change process, you will find your staff working efficiently in order to achieve the results and benefits that you promoted from the beginning of the process (Appelbaum et al., 2012).

You might find some elements that create hurdles in the journey of change. As a result, investigate these matters continuously, check for such hurdles and problems and, when discovered, eliminate them. By removing obstacles, you can empower and energize your journey towards change.

**Removing obstacles**. Appelbaum et al. (2012) made the following suggestions for action:

- Hire leaders who can play their role in promoting change
- Try to maintain checks and balances in your organization among associated departments so that your organization does not deviate from your vision
- Appreciate and reward those people who are promoting change with their positive efforts
- Strictly deal with those elements and people who are creating obstacles to making change occur
- Take immediate steps to remove obstacles

# Step Six: Create Short-term Wins

Success is the best key to inspiring people towards a cause. Try to give the pleasure of victory to the people of the company at various stages during the process of change. Within a brief time (i.e. a few months, contingent upon the nature of the change), you'll need to have accomplishments that your staff can see. If you fail to do so, fault-finders and critics can decrease your morale by criticizing your lack of progress. To do this, divide your process into intervals and targets. The systematic completion of each interval moves toward completion. This increases morale. People may need to work quite hard to accomplish their targets; however, each "win" propels the whole staff forward. It will also dissuade those critics.

> **How to create short-term wins.** Appelbaum et al. (2012) made the following suggestions for action:

- Try to choose targets that you can achieve in selected budgets and appropriate time
- Check for problems and their solutions on a regular basis
- Try to achieve success in early and alarming goals because if you fail to do so, then it may risk your change process
- Appreciate and award those who achieve their goals successfully

Dr. Radisha Brown

# Step Seven: Building Change

According to Kotter, announcing the victory too early is the reason behind the failure of some change processes. Genuine change runs profoundly. Speedy wins are just the start of necessary task requirements to accomplish long-term change.

Introducing one new item utilizing one new technique is incredibly effective (Appelbaum et al., 2012). In any case, when you can introduce 10 items, it is a sign of revving performance up to expectations. To achieve that tenth victory, you must continue looking for enhancements. Every victory gives a chance to expand on the processes that were successfully implemented.

**Ways to build change.** Appelbaum et al. (2012) made the following suggestions for action:

- Analyze the improvements which are required for change after achieving each success
- You should believe in the process of rapid and regular improvements
- Update your ideas by inviting new leaders into your journey of change

# Step Eight: Anchor the Change in the Corporate Culture

After implementing change, it is mandatory to make it stick by making it fundamental to your organization. Immediate steps should be taken to reflect the occurrence of change in all aspects of your organization (Appelbaum et al., 2012). Make sure that change is reflected in the corporate culture. Moreover, the management and key persons of the organization should favor the change, because if you lose the backing of these people, you may wind up back where you began.

**How to anchor change into the corporate culture.** Appelbaum et al. (2012) made the following suggestions for action:

- Discuss progress and prosperity frequently and demonstrate the successful stories of change
- Plan to swap key pioneers of change as they proceed onward, helping to guarantee that their legacy is not forgotten or disregarded
- Incorporate the change standards and qualities when procuring and preparing new staff

Dr. Radisha Brown

# Shields's Model

The Shields's (1999) model is based on the principle that endeavors to effect change primarily fail due to inadequate attention to the cultural and human aspects of business.

Sheilds pointed out that certain critical elements are required by leaders to bring about a change within an organization. The units within an organization are interlinked to a certain extent. Therefore, any type of change taking place in one business unit can lead to unproductive work processes if not aligned with other units.

This model amalgamates business process innovations with human resource management (Choi, 2011). It is imperative for the organizational management considering change to identify the strategies or the operations that are crucial to change. In addition, they must define the critical success factors before changing so that the degree to which the desired change can be accomplished is well communicated.

A number of models designed for organizational change do not incorporate this phase of change in their design. It is essential for organizational leaders to discuss the aims and objectives of the strategy for change with their employees.

If the goals of a planned change are not clearly communicated with the employees, the effort of change will be restricted to a series of unrelated change initiatives. Lastly, senior management should analyze the strengths of their workforce to determine the extent to which their employees can support the change process.

Sheilds (1999) proposed five steps that can lead to a successful change.

- **Step One** - Involves defining the expected outcomes and planning the process of change.

- **Step Two** - Establishes competency and potential to change.

- **Step Three** - Designs pioneering solutions.

- **Step Four** - Involves creating and implementing solutions.

- **Step Five** - Sustains and strengthens business benefits.

Dr. Radisha Brown

The Art of Storytelling

# Creating the Organizational Transition Plan for the Future

Defining the desired changes and fundamental reasons behind the change, along with the potential outcomes of the change, makes it simpler to create a successful organizational transition plan for the future. Whether the transition involves shifting to other locations or intends to take place in-house, designing a plan for all the phases of transition is crucial.

It facilitates measuring the performance of the change process against the goals. Hence, it is important to keep a continuous track record of all the steps that build the change process (Brusoni & Rosenkranz, 2014).

The steps involved in developing an organizational plan for the future are explained in detail below:

# Step 1

Critically assess the present state of an organization and identify the essential prerequisites. Examine the ongoing processes within the organization and identify those which

Dr. Radisha Brown

can be transitioned.

In the context of human resource management, the strategies (such as upgrading the human resource management system, improving the salaries and incentives) can be performed to transition the department (Brusoni & Rosenkranz, 2014).

Forecasting the outcomes of transition and identifying the potential requirements (for example introducing advanced technology or hiring skilled employees or commencing training programs) is essential but costly.

Therefore, organizations must plan smart and cost-effective strategies to assess the requirements of transition and its overall benefits.

# Step 2

Identify existing gaps and develop an understanding regarding the potential solutions to present and future demands. Align professionals with their respective process-related work-streams to assess every ongoing process. Determine the changes required in the future.

This includes the recruitment, performance management, and compensation processes; these must be revised to identify the potential requirements needed to be anticipated for the future (Brusoni & Rosenkranz, 2014).

# Step 3

Blueprint a proposal model that incorporates all the present and future transition demands. For example, if you are outsourcing your entire organization, then include the number of new hires, training programs, new location(s), cost and rent in the proposal model.

The design phase is assumed to be the most extensive phase of transition, but it is essential since it highlights the potential prospect requirements (Brusoni & Rosenkranz, 2014). It records the time span required for each stage of the transition process so that the approximate completion date of the transition project can be computed.

# Step 4

Put the approved plan into practice (for example, start hiring new staff, search for new locations and replace the outdated technologies with new ones).

# Step 5

Put the organizational transition in live mode. For example, move into the selected business center. Start the training of newly hired staff. Put the advanced technology into action.

Dr. Radisha Brown

The Art of Storytelling

# Impacts of Organizational Change

Often, an organization identifies a good business strategy and a good market positioning, but neglects the importance of assessing their impact, empowerment, and alignment of the organization with the new dynamics, including people, processes and technology, which could have negative affects Foth & Gray, 2009). It is at this point that organizational change arises.

At the moment the organization starts a program of change management, the organization should understand that the change program will ultimately impact corporate culture directly. Organizations adjusting to this scenario should map the impacts generated by the shift and move to a more focused and effective action.

These must align with the structure of the new company's organizational routine, focus on increasing performance and prepare the organization for the moment of change. Then the organization can react without losing control of the situation.

According to Barker and Gower (2010), many people will be affected directly or indirectly by a change in the organizational chart of a company. To these people, called stakeholders, this can be of a

Dr. Radisha Brown

legal or physical nature. Employees and other stakeholders influence the results and actions of the organization and are also influenced by them.

In this regard, organizational change "uninstalls" the employees, takes them out of their comfort zone and forces them to do things differently, which is not an easy task (Barker & Gower, 2010). Thus, it can be inferred that the overall process of change needs to be conducted carefully, surrounded by many cautious approaches so that employees feel the least possible discomfort. To meet these needs, from a systematic perspective, it is essential for the managers of the organizations to analyze different situations of the environment and, above all, recognize how different activities of the organizational process improve the situation.

Problems need to be recognized and corrected, preferably before they become critical. On the premise that there is a strong and powerful interdependence between the areas and sub-areas of an organization, and although the structure of the organization may permit a comfortable level of autonomy of the areas, a critical issue in one area can take an epidemiological nature, sprawling up to other areas.

> *One problem, originally, is always a problem, but that does not mean that, without being subjected to a proper form of treatment, it will not become a multitude of problems (Johansson & Heide, 2008).*

The Art of Storytelling

For a change to be implemented effectively, there are several factors which influence the organization when interacting with each other in the process. Characteristics and virtues are fundamental to these basic functions such as identifying the real significance of change, having the macro vision to influence its organized deployment in stages and  not becoming discouraged before problems arise  (Johansson & Heide, 2008).

Johansson & Heide believed that there are six specific aspects act as triggers for change:

- The nature of the labor force
- Technology
- Economic shocks
- Competition
- Social trends
- Political rends

To respond effectively to the demands of the environment, Johansson and Heide (2008) believed that organizations must also:

- Invest and worry about the increased quality and customer value
- Decrease costs of internal coordination
- Increase competitive innovation
- Reduce time-to-market
- Motivate members to contribute effectively
- Manage change fast
- Meet a real competitive advantage

For van Vuuren and Elving (2008), the factors capable of precipitating organizational changes are basically extra-organizational, i.e., changes in the business environment and economic recession.

Dr. Radisha Brown

However, other aspects must also be analyzed in a process change: organizational inertia, changes in organizational structure, and the environment in which it occurs. The causes or triggers of organizational change basically have two main sources: the external environment and the characteristics of the organization itself.

The following are issues connected to the external environment: the political world, crises and macroeconomic trends, legal and regulatory changes, economic recession, competition, and technological innovation. Characteristics of their own organization include: performance, personal characteristics of managers, the nature of the labor force, organizational growth and discontinuity in the organizational structure (van Vuuren & Elving, 2008).

The change must be in accordance with the organization's business, so it is necessary to make a strategic plan of the same type. The successful management of change depends largely on plans strategically developed and to view the plans as an ongoing process, not as a one-time event.

The plan is to understand the change process as a beginning, middle, and end, by stipulating goals and well-defined timelines. The power of change is a critical success factor for any organization (Powell, Elving, Dodd & Sloan, 2009).

The Art of Storytelling

# Understanding the Concept of Storytelling

"There has been re-emerging literature in the general field of management and leadership in business concerning the use of narratives to effectively communicate change" (Carriger, 2010, p. 305). In regard to change, Tichy and Cardwell (2002) wrote, "The best way to get humans to venture into unknown terrain is to make that terrain familiar and desirable by taking them there first in their imaginations" (p. 219).

From the early 1990s, several researchers have focused on the analysis of the phenomenon of *organizational communication* and its impact on human interactions, either internal or external in the organizations and how they influence organizational communications.

Powell, Elving, Dodd, and Sloan (2009) report that humans rely on language as a means of relating to and controlling their physical and social environment.

*Communication is defined as the glue that binds members, subunits, and organizations.*

Dr. Radisha Brown

The challenge in business is to provide employees with a clear message when communicating (Powell, Elving, Dodd & Sloan, 2009).

Organizational communication has two dominant interests: the skills that make for more efficient communication in individuals in their work, and the factors that characterize the communication efficiency in the system.

There are four major approaches to understanding organizational communication: (Love, 2008)

Communication as:
- transfer of information
- transactional process
- strategic control
- balance between creativity and constraint

The study of Mittins, Abratt, and Christie (2011) mentioned that storytelling has been used to pass down information throughout history. Although storytelling has been used for generations, there are steps required to successfully utilize stories during organizational change.

Briody (2012) discussed how an organization's culture is "solidified through tribal lore as members of each subgroup tell new members stories about life in the workplace" (p. 68). These stories can reflect positive or negative images of an organization as well as impact an employee's dedication to the organization.

Simmons (2006) related that "stories move people to a very young state of awareness that is less analytical, more receptive, and better connected to their unconscious and imagination" (p. 126).

The Art of Storytelling

Storytelling's power comes from the speaker's ability to tell the story and to connect with the audience. O'Leary, Choi, and Gerard (2012) related that "great storytellers build a mental picture in the mind of the audience, based on their needs, history, and experience (p. 9).

Stories have the ability to inspire, connect and drive people to action (Silverman, 2006). Silverman wrote that stories, when linked to business objectives, quickly accelerate the work and increase collaboration among team members.

In this fast-paced economy, organizations must find ways to quickly and effectively communicate with staff members. The purpose of this paper is to explore the use of storytelling as a tool for leaders to communicate corporate strategy throughout the organization.

At the very outset, it is important to understand the concept of storytelling as a communication tool. In organizations, storytelling has become an effective communication tool to share real-life experiences, stories, knowledge, and narratives to develop a positive organizational culture in the organization.

Communication is an integral part of the positive and learning organizational culture. Storytelling and communication are interlinked tools that are used in the organization for achieving a positive transformation.

The studies by Festing (2012) and Ribiere and Sitar (2003) indicated that storytelling is about sharing experiences that have a moral for all the employees. It is a strong story with a strong message

Dr. Radisha Brown

to convey the organizational objectives or vision.

The message is the most important element of storytelling, which helps in directing the behavior of employees in the organization. It is the role of an effective leader who builds an organizational culture where storytelling is used as a communication tool to motivate and encourage employees. The behavior and attitude of employees are changed through effective storytelling.

According to Dailey and Browning (2013), storytelling is the same storytelling that children love to hear. Similarly, at the workplace, storytelling helps by enhancing the emotional connection between the leader and the organization itself. It was further highlighted by Gill (2011) that storytelling is about sharing the values and norms of the organization so that they are understood clearly by all the employees.

Furthermore, it has been highlighted by the study of Auvinen, Aaltio, and Blomqvist (2013) that storytelling is used in organizations as a means of building mutual trust and understanding. This results in a positive organizational culture where employees are willing to work. Therefore, successful organizational change is dependent upon the willingness and flexibility of employees.

The willingness and flexibility of employees can only be achieved by building motivation and inspiration through storytelling. Storytelling is used for inspiring and motivating the employees towards accelerated performance and efficiency.

According to Bowman, MacKay, Masrani and McKiernan (2013), communication is the catalyst for enhancing the engagement and commitment of stakeholders towards achieving positive organizational change.

In the contemporary business environment, change has become an important aspect for meeting the new demands of the market. Change is needed to achieve responsiveness and efficiency, which are the key aspects of survival and growth in the present age. Therefore, innovative communication tools are required to influence and encourage employees towards organizational change. It is important to understand change occurs due to the impact of macro and micro forces.

These environmental forces play an important role in bringing organizational change. Organizational change becomes inevitable and requires the role of leaders to initiate positive change in the organization. Therefore, the most effective communication tool for minimizing the barriers to positive change is storytelling and narratives.

New companies are created daily through a desire, a market insight, or an internal process innovation (Mittins, Abratt & Christie, 2011). Each has its peculiarities from its inception. Today, the public does not want to only buy products. They want to "talk" with the brands. Customers want to feel they are a part of the brand's story, development, banners, etc.

In this new scenario, it is important to promote ways to engage the customer in various media and wrap it with branding concepts in various contexts.

Dr. Radisha Brown

> *Commotion Through Emotion*
>
> *The main purpose of organizations using storytelling is to gather the stories of the company and tell them to the public in a way that causes a commotion.*

People are accustomed to hearing histories over time; stories that are perpetuated in our lives precisely by culture and habits of ancestorsPfeffermann, 2011). Today, with the ease of sharing content on the internet, individuals have many opportunities and platforms to tell these stories in the digital environment.

But there is a difference between children's stories and business stories: Unlike the storytelling model for children, where imagination can flow without necessarily having ties with reality, the exact opposite happens with companies.

A well-told story can truly convey what happened to that organization, from its beginning to its development during all the years of existence. This is how organizations begin to create more connection with the audience.

With the advent of the use of this information through various communication channels and media, the intelligence in the storytelling of these stories and the way it is involved in these channels will make a difference over competitors (Tobin & Snyman, 2008).

The Art of Storytelling

# CHAPTER 14

# Using Storytelling as a Communication Tool for Organizational Change

It has become crucial for organizations to focus on effective communication to enhance performance and job satisfaction. For achieving positive organizational change, it is important to have minimal resistance to change.

As per Mittins, Abratt, and Christie (2011), storytelling works as a useful communication tool for minimizing the resistance to change through motivational stories. The stories are told to remove misunderstandings and resistance through real-life examples and inspirational stories. It is important for the leader to have a charismatic and influential leadership style for achieving the effectiveness of storytelling as a communication tool.

In the context of various studies, storytelling has become a phenomenal communication tool for organizational change. In recent years, many organizations have adopted storytelling as a communication tool for enhancing the process of organizational change.

Storytelling greatly helps organizations to enhance their

Dr. Radisha Brown

change programs. With the help of storytelling, many organizations are now able to effectively communicate with both their internal and external stakeholders when they plan to bring about any organizational change.

For example, if an organization aims to bring a change to the overall organizational culture, then it can successfully communicate with its employees through storytelling. The organization can use storytelling as a communication tool to inform its employees about the new change incentive.

Storytelling has made the communication process highly interesting and interactive. When an organization tries to communicate or convey a message through a story, the audience listens with more interest.

Organizational psychologists have observed that human beings are nurtured with the concept of listening to stories since their childhood; therefore, they have developed a taste and interest in listening to stories with a high level of interest. With the emergence of storytelling as a communication tool, the task of bringing organizational change has become extremely easy for organizations. Human beings tend to enjoy things with which they have prior experience, such as listening to stories since their childhood.

> *Human beings tend to enjoy things with which they have prior experience, such as listening to stories since their childhood.*

The Art of Storytelling

Direct and boring forms of communication through which an organization informs its audience do not have any significant impact in terms of influencing them. Conversely, through storytelling, organizations not only develop the interest of their audience but also influence them to a significant extent.

Storytelling does not only make the change process easy for the organization but also for the audience. The stories are told to remove misunderstandings and resistance through real-life examples and inspirational stories.

It is important for the leader to have a charismatic and influential leadership style for achieving the effectiveness of storytelling as a communication tool. For example, if the organization intends to implement a change in the organizational structure, then the employees would be able to understand it more clearly if they are told about it in the form of a story rather than in the form of a direct statement.

It is imperative for organizations to understand that the human resources of the organization play an integral role in achieving the success of the change process. The employees are the key towards the successful implementation of a change program.

> *The employees are the key towards the successful implementation of a change program.*

Therefore, it is highly important for organizations to successfully communicate the change plan to its employees before

Dr. Radisha Brown

undertaking any action because, without the contribution of the employees, the change plan can never achieve its true goal.

Many organizational psychologists have also pointed out that, at times, the change process is extremely easy, but the task of communicating and convincing the employees to take part in the process becomes extremely difficult. Therefore, with the advent of storytelling as a communication tool, organizations can successfully tackle this problem by not only building the interest of the employees in the change program, but by also convincing them to effectively and positively contribute towards its success.

The process of using storytelling as a communication tool, however, is not as easy as it seems. The organization needs to work extensively toward developing an interesting story that relates to the new organizational change plan. Hence, the story should not only be interesting, but should also be directly related to the new change plan of the organization.

Organizations need to cover both aspects of communication; that is, it should communicate interestingly so that the employees do not get bored and, secondly, the organization should relate the change plan in their storytelling.

Storytelling has become a popular communication tool in recent years, mainly because it greatly minimizes resistance to change. This is because, when employees are informed about the forthcoming change process in an autocratic and dry manner, they usually perceive the change in a negative sense and are reluctant to participate in the process. However, with the help of storytelling, it has become much easier for organizations to positively influence their employees to participate in the change process.

As a result, storytelling has greatly reduced the problem of resistance to change and many organizations have started adopting this new concept in implementing successful organizational changes in a positive and effective manner.

With the advent of globalization, the business environment has been transformed in terms of increased competition and consumerism. More and more organizations are emerging in the global markets and are challenging each other by trying to gain the maximum market share and profitability.

It has become critically important for all organizations to keep up to date with the latest trends, innovations, and changes. If an organization lags in any aspect, then its market share is immediately snatched away by its rival competitor.

In order to avoid this, it has become essential for all organizations to focus on effective communication and change implementation and to achieve both simultaneously. In this scenario, the concept of storytelling has emerged. With the help of storytelling, organizations can effectively communicate and bring meaningful changes to retain their market share and competitiveness in the global business environment.

Storytelling has emerged as a powerful communication tool for bringing a positive organizational change. This tool is gaining more and more popularity due to its various benefits that are greatly benefiting the diverse business environment of the 21$^{st}$ century.

Dr. Radisha Brown

According to Geiger and Schreyögg (2012), storytelling as a communication tool is used for several major purposes.

**Storytelling used for sharing norms and values of the organization.**

Stories are used for communicating the norms and values of the organization. The organizational culture is a developed through these norms and values, which are the foundation of the organization. It is the role of a strong leader who can bring effective communication to the organization to pave the way for positive organizational culture. The values and norms of the organization need to be communicated to the employees so that they follow the same footsteps and vision that the organization aims to achieve. It is vital to bridge the gap between the interests of the organization and the employees to create a harmonious relationship where the values and norms of the organization are respected.

It is important to note that powerful and dominant stories of the organization play a significant role in increasing the level of adaptation of employees towards organizational norms and values. These norms and values are highly important for achieving the long-term vision and mission of the organization.

**Storytelling used for developing mutual trust and commitment with the organization.**

Leaders use stories to communicate their competencies and commitment with oneself and the organization. This makes storytelling a source of inspiration and commitment for employees. It is important to understand that mutual trust and commitment are the most important aspects for achieving a positive organizational culture.

In today's highly competitive environment, organizations try to retain resourceful employees for gaining and keeping the long-term competitive advantage. This long-term competitive advantage can only be achieved through efficient and competent human resources of the organization. The human resource is the real asset of the organization, for it is they who can help in achieving accelerated performance while facing critical challenges and complexities. It requires immense effort to build and sustain a competitive advantage through efficient and competent human resources.

Communication tools play a major role in enhancing the mutual trust and commitment of employees. In times of organizational transformation, this trust and commitment need to be retained through storytelling.

Dr. Radisha Brown

**Storytelling is used for sharing knowledge to improve the capabilities and awareness of employees for accepting organizational change.**

Knowledge sharing is one of the objectives of using storytelling as a communication tool for organizations. Today, organizations are operating in highly volatile and complex markets, which require adaptability and responsiveness to meet the needs of the market. Therefore, organizational redesigning and organizational change have become inevitable and require effective communication tools to retain employees' commitment and performance.

Organizational change is not welcomed by employees due to the restructuring and redesigning which alters the work processes and roles of employees. However, change is necessary in order to adopt the approach of continuous learning. In contemporary organizations, continuous learning is followed by organizational change when required to meet the needs of the market. Communication tools are used by the organization to create a flexible, adaptive and earning organizational culture for organizational change.

Venkitachalam and Busch (2012) and Whyte and Classen (2012) portrayed stories as a tiny fuse that detonates tacit understanding in the mind of the listener. It is important to understand that tacit and experience-based knowledge needs to be emphasized for influencing employees. Learning and unlearning process can only be made effective through storytelling, which focuses on tacit knowledge and understanding.

As per Rosile, Boje, Carlon, Downs, and Saylors (2013), storytelling facilitates learning and capacity building for accomplishing positive organizational change. Stories have the capacity to achieve employee engagement which helps in effective communication. Stories engage employees in the organization's culture and values, which ultimately helps in bringing positive change into the organization.

Several studies such as Boal and Schultz (2007), have indicated storytelling is a forceful communication tool that develops strong emotional connections within the organization. Employees feel part of the organization when the leader relates the story with their experiences, grievances, and challenges. This helps to build an emotional and practical bond which is based on workplace problems and challenges.

When organizational changes are expected, employees feel insecure and unwilling to perform well (Harris & Barnes, 2006). Therefore, storytelling becomes an effective communication tool for minimizing the resistance and misunderstandings of the employees. The emotional connection helps in regenerating the commitment and engagement of employees towards accelerated performance and efficiency. Therefore, storytelling has become a key communication tool for achieving positive organizational change.

When the techniques of storytelling are used in a proper and effective manner, they are an important complement to the purely rational, formal and technical model attempt to involve others and constitute valuable tools of persuasion.

Every organization, as it evolves, accumulates a series of experiences, cases and learning experiences associated with leaders and teams while at work in operations and projects. Technical challenges, markets, and management are overcome and often end up embedded in operational processes, documents, software patents and the organization (Tobin & Snyman, 2008). This type of explicit knowledge, however, does not carry the contexts, values and personal stories that helped in the evolution of the organization.

Stories, in turn, are rich in these elements. The values of an organization live largely in the stories that are told, relived and remembered every moment and have permeated the lives of organizations. Every organization has its stories of war heroes and their worldviews constructed from large or small anecdotes that convey daily and perpetuate the ethos of the organization.

Finally, the values of an organization live in the stories that are told, remembered and relived. Shared in moments of spontaneous or deliberately to emphasize some sort of behavior desired. (Pfeffermann, 2011). Most of the stories in an organization

The Art of Storytelling

are based on real cases, which can be modified slightly for emphasis on a specific point or to drive the narrative.

**Some examples of types of stories in the organizational context are:**

- **Inspirational Stories** are used to stimulate the imagination and generate energy and cooperation;

- **Preventative Action Stories** are used to teach lessons about the danger from certain negative emotions or insecurities, and

- **Culture Building Stories** are used to reflect a specific organizational value, such as loyalty, trust, always prioritizing the client, sustainability, etc.

# Storytelling is a way to use the narrative to share knowledge, experiences, and information.

As a new trend in business, storytelling has been used in this context to rescue and preserve the memory of a company as well as being a motivator and a way to strengthen values and culture. Allied to communication and marketing tools, storytelling has gained ground in business by being a simple tool that stirs the most important part of organizations, i.e., its people.

Storytelling, like any form of communication, should be done with the help of proper planning (Kearney, 2011). Organizations and

Dr. Radisha Brown

their management must identify the communication objectives, and then map the existing stories that meet these goals and seek to understand how best to tell these stories.

The concept of storytelling works effectively to convey any form of message. Storytelling is effective in communication because the act of storytelling, which is so simple and yet so persuasive, can join popular culture, public participation and dreamed recognition. Storytelling is a feature of communication that uses narratives to approach organizing your most important audiences.

According to Blundel and Ippolito (2008), telling stories in the organization and about the organization has an important role in the life of any person because it brings "meaning". That's because the lived experience is a powerful resource to empathize and differentiate the organization from the many thousands of demands that are out there.

This tool supports initiatives to gain supporters and fundraisers because it provides differentiation and can attract and engage audiences using the power that narrative must approach from experiences. Storytelling can be applied in multiple, creative and inexpensive ways, working from stories of the brand and its stakeholders (Kearney, 2011).

Storytelling is a tool much used nowadays in companies aiming to create a connection between leaders and their teams. Although there are numerous definitions for the term, such as the ability to develop logical thinking and provide the receiver of the message a full understanding of the situation described, storytelling is the oldest way of telling stories (Kearney, 2011). Storytelling favors the understanding of complex issues and helps translate strategy into action. This permits professionals to have an in-depth and clear idea about their objectives ⟨OBJ⟩ (Mládková, 2012).

The organizational narrative has both an individual and collective role. The individual role serves to make the individual feel part of a culture. A collective role is an active tool of communication and engagement, able to convey an inspiring message. Through stories, lessons from the past begin to make sense and the future possibilities become clearer (Kearney, 2011). In companies, the tool can manifest itself in various ways, through strategic decisions, values, business practices, and methods of addressing stakeholders, among others.

Storytelling is a set of communication techniques that has existed since language was created, between 30 and 100 thousand years ago.

**The concept of storytelling can be used in different situations such as:**

- Knowledge management - identification and exchange of knowledge

- Organizational culture - exploring values, create a collective vision and inspire people towards change when necessary

- Communication - balancing quantitative information with qualitative evidence, based on real examples

- Teams, networks, and communities - to create strong

connections, integrate new professionals in the environment and share common purposes

- Risk management - to manage uncertainty and develop a look ahead among professionals

According to Blundel and Ippolito (2008), "storytelling" is used in the context of organizations as a tool to expand the strategic vision of teams, processes and markets. This is because traditional oral narrative depends on personal experience, the imagination of the storyteller and the receiver is impacted by reason and emotion.

Thus, any good story can contain conflict and its outputs, with figures and examples. At present, the concept of storytelling is becoming increasingly significant and important in corporate communication, mainly in relation to the employees. Fast growth, decentralized organization, and different languages and cultures make it difficult to convey the values and identity of the company (Whyte & Classen, 2012).

Corporate storytelling facilitates communication. Basically, corporate storytelling uses narrative elements in communication via metaphors, practical examples, and culturally-rooted gender roles.

When engaged in corporate storytelling, a distinction is made between two types of stories, i.e., grounding stories and instructional stories.

**Grounding stories** are used to convey the "key values" (key messages, corporate values) of the organization.

**Instructional stories** explain the procedures and processes in the company to employees (Whyte & Classen, 2012).

The Art of Storytelling

The overall objective is the sustainable development of a tangible identity in the organization. Therefore, storytelling is an effective management communication tool for all organizations. Stories have always been used as a tool to teach values, norms, or legal measures.

Stories are not just for entertainment, but to fulfill a function: Stories convey information in an exciting, easy to understand package. Corporate storytelling is the use of stories as a management tool (Whyte & Classen, 2012).

Dr. Radisha Brown

The Art of Storytelling

# CHAPTER 15

# Contexts where Storytelling is a Useful Communication Tool

Storytelling as a communication tool is useful in the following kinds of contexts. According to Sole and Wilson (2002), the major kinds of contexts in which storytelling as a communication tool is useful are initiating a new idea, interacting with new employees, improving relationships, managing resistance to change and sharing wisdom.

First, initiating a new idea is the context in which storytelling is useful. New ideas and innovations require influencing skills of the leader for achieving adaptability. New ideas are linked with organizational changes, which ultimately require leadership skills to implement. The phases from idea generation to final testing and implementation require effective communication in the organization to align the functional activities and interests of all stakeholders. It is important to note that during changes, there is a need for developing and retaining the trust level and commitment of employees to achieve the end goal.

According to Harris and Barnes (2006), it becomes crucial for management to sustain a positive internal culture and the

Dr. Radisha Brown

performance level of employees during the initiation of new ideas and concepts in the organization. Storytelling is based on compelling and emotional stories that create a strong bond between the employees and organization to work together during organizational change for achieving commonly shared objectives.

Second, storytelling is useful when interacting with new employees in the organization. As per Varga (2012), the new employees entering the organization need to be informed about its values, norms, and culture.

Storytelling serves as an effective communication tool to guide the new employees towards the organization. It helps in explaining the informal and formal activities and works in the organization in which it is being practiced. Storytelling is a method of sharing cultural values and norms with the new employees.

It helps in socialization and relationship building in the organization, which paves the way for a positive organizational culture. Basically, storytelling is used as an effective and efficient effective method of internal communication, but in many cases, the potential is now also applied to recruitment.

Storytelling is entering organizations, either as an internal communication strategy or as a recruitment and selection tool. The concept is simple, experts say (paraphrased): it is about telling a story in a strategic way that transmits values and knowledge that builds the image and reputation of a company, brand, or candidate.

Third, storytelling helps maintain and improve relationships in the organization for achieving positive organizational change and accelerated performance. Narrative therapy has been used for mending relationships. Similarly, storytelling helps minimize misunderstandings and bridges gaps between individuals (Rosile, Boje, Carlon, Downs & Saylors, 2013). In organizations, relationships play a critical role in achieving performance, innovation, efficiency and positive change. The transformation towards growth and progress can only be achieved through maintaining and sustaining positive relationships in the organization.

Finally, storytelling is useful when wisdom and knowledge must be shared for enhancing the potential and competencies of individuals. Knowledge and wisdom from seniors and experienced leaders play a strong role in enhancing the engagement and motivation of employees towards accepting change in the organization. Communication and organizational change are interlinked to achieve long-term objectives of the organization.

Storytelling is one of the most effective tools for communicating with employees where the leader can play the role of a mentor. Mentoring through storytelling plays a highly influential role in achieving positive organizational change.

Mentoring is reflected in storytelling where the mentor aims to guide individuals in times of organizational change and transformation. The interests and career goals of employees are matched with the objectives of the organization so that common goals can be identified and communicated to the employees. This helps in building a positive attitude and direction in the organization for organizational change. It becomes important to have the right

Dr. Radisha Brown

direction for bringing positive outcomes for both the employees and the organization.

Therefore, every organization, since its inception, has an identity and becomes part of a story. This story is constructed from a range of experiences and visions related to internal and external relations of their daily events. When connected to a professional organization that offers a product or service to a customer, giving examples and telling stories is a technique called storytelling (van Vuuren & Elving, 2008). This technique uses the stories and narratives as a tool for communication and education, favoring the achievement of results.

But the storytelling technique could be used for representing organizations in modern times. We live in a society where information is increasingly abundant, and the reality is that people's attention is increasingly scarce. There is the impression that we walked into a rhythm of life whose feeling is that it seems impossible to monitor everything that happens around the world around us. The longstanding mode of storytelling is an innovative form of communication that is used by various organizations and can also be used by any professional, in various situations such as meetings, personal conversations, public presentations, negotiations or sales (Pfeffermann, 2011).

The professional can engage your customers, your staff, your employees and partners through an open form of communication. The power of narratives and histories, internal and external communication, is becoming a more effective way to interact,

The Art of Storytelling

135 P a g e

motivate, and become close, being empathetic and practice otherness in the corporate world. In other words, telling a good story is the shortest way to get someone's attention.

Although it is quiet and easy, the gift of creating a story that really attracts the attention of your viewers is a complex process. It requires a large investment of time, which is already an increasingly scarce element in our society (Hearn, Foth & Gray, 2009).

Given this concern, the big key to practice so that storytelling works is to make use of a story that is unique, real, and above all, exclusively able to convey a strong position, leading to gaining the trust of the viewer making him feel motivated. In this sense, humans have been proficient storytellers for thousands of years. In our daily life, there is no one who does not consume stories in one way or another, either through film, novel, and literature or even in an everyday environment with friends, colleagues, etc.

We act and position ourselves when facing a situation or context based on the values we have for what we see, hear and experience. In the case of storytelling, it can be a great motivational technique to harness this potential to bring people together through the meanings and values that they share to gain their trust and show them how you can make a difference.

Thus, if someone knows and recounts a really good story, the audience will react positively. The act of storytelling cannot only change, but shape the world's perception of what the other holds to be true (Pfeffermann, 2011).

Dr. Radisha Brown

The Art of Storytelling

# Storytelling in Managing Knowledge

According to Kankainen, Vaajakallio, Kantola, and Mattelmäki (2012), storytelling seems to be something natural, particularly for great leaders. Despite that, until recently, administrative science paid little attention to this phenomenon. This is changing both in theory and in practice. In the context of knowledge management (as well as certain frustration with large projects, modification of knowledge and transfer of knowledge by means of information technology), there is recognition of the crucial importance of stories to transfer knowledge of complex contexts, visions, and cultural values.

Storytelling is a technique that enhances multiple causal relationships. It is multi-faceted, stimulates both the right side as well as the left side of the brain and allows those who read or hear the story to strongly engage with it - dreaming, acting and reflecting as the story evolves. This form, the experience and the lessons learned, are transmitted to establish meaning, elicit emotion and serve as standard or archetype for future decision making or action in similar situations (Whyte & Classen, 2012).

The method of storytelling in the organizational context of

Dr. Radisha Brown

Knowledge Management was introduced in a deliberate and systematic manner and has been effectively used by various organizations, such as the World Bank, NASA, Johnson & Johnson, Conoco, Boeing, etc. In these companies, storytelling is not just seen as a distraction or relaxation time (although it can also cause this effect). It is one of the institutional tools or methods in the context of Knowledge Management (Tobin & Snyman, 2008).

How does the method of storytelling compare to other methods normally associated with Knowledge Management? To what extent is the method of storytelling effective when it comes to transferring knowledge? Storytelling does more than transfer specific knowledge, it transfers values and attitudes. It helps build commitments to future visions. If the main goal is to transfer specific technical knowledge, standards, and best practices, other methods are more appropriate.

In this sense, storytelling is more an instrument for those involved with Knowledge Management (Mládková, 2012). The novelty is that in more recent times, storytelling is being quite instrumental in the context of teams, departments, and even organizations, seeking profound changes, the transfer of attitudes, ways of addressing challenges, as well as methods for dealing with complex situations.

The Art of Storytelling

# Summary

# Summary of Organizational Change

To this point, this chapter discussed the relevant literature related to the topic. The literature review was designed to effectively answer the research questions discussed in the first chapter of the dissertation. The chapter presented an overview of the company that is the focus of this dissertation and highlighted its operational strategies. The chapter then highlighted widely used definitions of change and reasons that lead to the change process.

At present, the majority of organizations across the globe function under escalating demands for change. The marketplace has changed drastically due to high competition, technological advancement, increased customer demands and globalization. This rapidity in change requires that organizations change their behaviors and policies to effectively acclimate and compete with shifts in the market.

Organizational change refers to demands placed on organizational subunits that require a significant departure from employees' current routines and behaviors. The success of change

Dr. Radisha Brown

depends upon the support of those affected. Change is a constant; therefore, organizations must be prepared to address all changes. Organizational change is a process through which an organization optimizes its productivity and performance to acquire an ideal position in the market.

Organizational change occurs in organizations because they must adapt to keep up with changes in the external business environment. The need for organizational change might also arise to address crisis situations. According to a proactive approach, a change is an initiation by the senior management of an organization to enhance the performance of the organization. Various researchers were reviewed for aspects of change concerned with the various threats and challenges faced by contemporary organizations today.

These include challenges from turbulent environments, threats to efficiency and effectiveness, increased competency levels and alternating customer demands. All these factors acquire great significance in keeping companies viable and healthy. The process of organizational change is not automatic; it requires proper planning for the desired change and designing effective strategies to manage the change. Successful organizations respond sharply to factors which precipitate change.

Implementing a change is a very difficult process, especially when employees and stakeholders resist change. Resistance to change is defined as the process through which the employees oppose change. Resistance to change is assumed to be one of the most significant factors that influence the success of an

The Art of Storytelling

organizational change that encompasses new policies, the latest organizational structure, and technological advancement. Frequently, resistance to change is so destructive to change endeavors that the efforts made to address the contributing factors form the bedrock of managing the change.

Resistance to change is a natural process and takes place when employees do not accept the desired change. Employees resist change because they want things to stay the same. They believe that the planned change can adversely affect them. Therefore, it is essential for senior management to effectively communicate the mission and vision of the planned changed with their employees and encourage them to participate in the change process. Organizational change can take place in different forms.

Change can be invasive or non-invasive, planned or unplanned, and episodic or continuous. Each type incorporates different working principals. This chapter presented different models for organizational change but focused on models presented by Shields, Kotter, and Lewin. The Shields model for organizational change consists of five steps. Kotter's model put forward eight steps to successfully implement a change. The Lewin's Three-Step Model comprises three steps that are Unfreeze, Transition, and Freeze.

All these models effectively bring about the desired change within an organization. To effectively lead the change, identify the reasons that trigger change and design a corresponding response to those factors. To successfully accomplish the goals of change, it is essential for the change agents to be equipped with the skills needed to effectively guide subordinates through organizational change.

O'Leary et al (2012) wrote that "more than communication, storytelling is the art of combining verbal and nonverbal information to communicate a specific message that creates credibility, adds value, is easy to understand, and engages the audience" (p. 2).

The literature supports the theoretical framework contained in this research that storytelling can be an effective tool for implementing organizational change when used properly. O'Leary et al. examined the responses of 200 employees who were presented with information on the company's strategy change either through a meeting and power point presentation or a story. The employees were given surveys asking them to recall the reasons for the strategy change. The goal of this research was to provide statistical data showing the effectiveness of using stories to communicate strategy change.

In summary, as Paden (2011) stated, "storytelling helps to register, summarize, and allow reconstruction of scenarios that are too complex for logical linear summaries to preserve (p. 96). Storytelling is a singular act in the form of narration, constituting a language persuasive in communication (Salmon 2007).

Storytelling is not a simple narrative but a process to persuade listeners. The most important Business storytelling has its roots in branding (brand management). We have discovered the power of abstraction of a brand, "which seemed to be of fundamental importance, since corporations may manufacture products, but what consumers buy are brands." Brands like Nike,

The Art of Storytelling

Apple, The Body Shop, Calvin Klein, Disney, Levi's and Starbucks are increasingly engaged in the act of branding.

Driven by consumer capitalism, the advertisements began appropriating the myths, legends, tales, epics, novels, i.e., the collective saga of humanity. For Mládková (2012), advertising creates brands wrapping products into our dreams and fantasies, wraps products with identity, personalities, and sensibilities that reflect our own values and sensibilities.

The trend is that organizations face difficulties in attracting public interest. Storytelling has a great importance because it attracts attention. Therefore, within the context of IC (Internal Communication), the storytelling mode can be used as a strategic communication tool. Storytelling becomes one of the most viable tools for companies that have difficulties capturing the attention of their employees or making them understand the whole organization's principles, values, and history.

As a communication tool, storytelling facilitates the understanding between organizations and their employees through communication and knowledge sharing. It creates an organizational style and identity through emotional involvement by motivating employees, making them feel vital and an important part of the group (Tobin & Snyman, 2008).

This is an effective communication tool that helps employees achieve their goals in an effective manner and generates revenue for the organization through selling techniques: An organization can, for instance, tell a story in which their product or service is the hero. A

Dr. Radisha Brown

manager can encourage their team with a history demonstrating that individual or continuous efforts generate success.

Storytelling may seem simple, but it is a powerful and effective communication tool for organizational change. It is the transmission of events in words, images, and sounds, often by improvisation or stories with narratives that include plot, characters and narrative point of view. The term storytelling has long been used in the communication strategies of brands, as businesses increasingly use this tool to create emotions and desires in the heart and mind of consumers. It is important to remember, however, that the art of storytelling is a process that must begin long before the creation of a campaign.

The construction of the history of a brand goes mainly through the process of creating a personal connection between consumers and the company. This connection only occurs when this story creates a feeling around what the company does, creating empathy that leads to interaction between brand and business, sharing belief in the same style, the same values, and the same worldviews.

Storytelling is a strong tool for communicating both internally and externally (Whyte & Classen, 2012). Projects are communicated and messages are transmitted through stories, creating an emotional bond, facilitating understanding and memorization. The concept of storytelling has become a phenomenal communication tool for organizational change.

In recent times, several organizations have adopted

The Art of Storytelling

storytelling as the tool of communication for improving and enhancing the overall procedure of organizational change. Storytelling assists organizations to improve their overall programs of change (Tobin & Snyman, 2008).

With the help of storytelling, many organizations are now able to effectively communicate with both their internal and external stakeholders when they plan to bring about any organizational change.

The organization can use storytelling as a communication tool to inform its employees about the new change incentive. Storytelling has made the communication process highly interesting and interactive. When an organization tries to communicate or convey a message through a story, the audience listens with more interest (Kearney, 2011).

Dr. Radisha Brown

The Art of Storytelling

# METHODOLOGY

This chapter describes the methodology used in this study. It details the overall methodology and approach, research design, participant selection, population and sampling, qualitative instrument, field testing, data collection and analysis, researcher's critical analysis of design, reliability, and validity, ethical considerations.

Dr. Radisha Brown

The Art of Storytelling

CHAPTER

# Research Design

This study used a qualitative approach to data collection and analysis. Qualitative research aims at the essence of a research problem to gain and understand a new and personal point of view. In contrast, quantitative research aims at the scientific reality and applicability to practice. The most noteworthy difference between qualitative and quantitative research is that the former is subjective, and the latter is objective.

The subjectiveness of the qualitative data can be weighed by the fact that it produces rich and deep data (Broom, 2007). On the other hand, quantitative research methodology focuses on the countable, repeatable, and statistical analysis of data. Both, however, involve the interpretation of results by the researcher. The qualitative method usually gives non-generalizable results, because the information is in-depth and applicable only to an area under discussion. The quantitative model produces data that is generalizable.

The formulation and interpretation of the research problem are common in both models. Both the research models require data collection, data interpretation, and data analysis strategies. Quantitative research requires the use of similar statistical and

Dr. Radisha Brown

numerical data representation tools such as count sheets, control charts, pie- charts, histograms, etc. Qualitative data typically does not. In qualitative research, in-depth verbatim interviews help in the construal implication of results (Caelli, 2002).

This study used a qualitative methodology research design. Qualitative research methodology allowed the flexibility necessary for gaining an in-depth understanding of participants' experiences of the use of storytelling to communicate organizational change.

# Subjects

There were 9 participants, 3 females and 6 males. The participants work in the wholesale trade sector, health care, and transportation industries. All participants work fulltime and live in either the Augusta, Georgia or Charlotte, North Carolina areas. Of the total 9 participants, 7 interviews were conducted in person while 2 were telephone interviews.

# Instrumentation

The goal of qualitative research is to create an environment where participants feel comfortable opening up about potentially sensitive information. In-depth interviews are a common strategy in obtaining and analyzing the behaviors, opinions, arguments, and experiences of the research participants. When conducting in-depth interviews, it is important for the researcher to remain focused on the research topic and questions. This researcher abstained from

The Art of Storytelling

using biased language that would impact participant responses. The discussions with each participant were transcribed during the individual interviews.

During the analytic phase of the research, this researcher coded and categorized the responses using software designed to summarize transcriptions. This process involved recognizing any patterns or themes about the research subject and removing any irrelevant data. The original data, as well as the data used to summarize, is included in the appendix portion of the research paper.

# Process

Primary data were collected by the researcher through participant interviews. Primary data holds immense importance as it is first-hand data collected by the researcher to explore the research questions. All participant views are subjective and have equally merited interpretations (Kachel & Jennings, 2010). Goldkuhl (2012) stated, "The aims of understanding the subjective meanings of persons in studied domains are essential in the interpretive paradigm" (p. 137).

The primary data in this study were collected through one-on-one interviews. The interview questions consisted of:

1. Can you explain what is storytelling?

2. Can you describe what you believe are the important features of storytelling?

3. What has been your experience with your organization using storytelling to communicate

Dr. Radisha Brown

organizational change?

4.  Describe your feelings about organizations using storytelling to communicate change?

5.  Tell me what you think about storytelling encouraging full engagement of employees?

6.  What advice would you give your leader about using storytelling to communicate organizational change?

Secondary data were collected using already-available data. The researcher extracted data from online sources and used that to explore the research questions. Therefore, the data were collected in a sequential manner where the researcher ensured that the research instrument used for collection of primary data was reliable in achieving research aims and objectives.

This section describes the methods and procedures for data collection. Prior to data being collected, this researcher attained Argosy University's Institutional Review Board's written approval to conduct interviews. Once approval was given, this research began conducting interviews.

**Field Testing.** Interviewing participants on the surface appears to be straightforward because the interviewer is tasked with asking questioning and giving participants the opportunity to answer the questions. However, interviewing can become quite difficult when conducted in a formal setting, in which novice interviewers may feel awkward and must monitor how they handle the actual interview process (Hannabuss, 1996). Field testing provides an excellent method to ensure that the questions developed will be relevant, clearly understandable and provides usable data.

Field testing allowed this researcher to improve her interviewing skills. This researcher has prior experience in performing client evaluations for medical and mental health assessments, which are typically closed-ended questions. However, this research required a slightly different process to ensure that the interviews were structured but allowed flexibility. Field testing was conducted using practice interviews with co-workers. No data were collected during the field testing process; however, participants will be providing feedback and suggestions for improvements.

The field testing allowed this researcher to perform proactive interviews with three individuals to determine if the chosen research questions, structure, and intended interview process were appropriate for the study. The first test interviewee reported that this researcher "did not provide eye conduct during the entire interview and it made her feel uncomfortable at times." The second interviewee related that this researcher should remove the word "more" from the interview question, which stated, "Tell me more about storytelling encouraging full engagement of employees." The third test interviewee stated, "these questions caused me to have to think really hard about the way that my company communicates with employees." Additionally, the third pilot test participant recommended that this researcher allocate 60 minutes for each interview to ensure that respondents do not feel rushed. The

Dr. Radisha Brown

feedback received during the field testing were used to improve and finalize the interview process.

Seidman's (2006) three phase interview approach was used to collect the data. The approach provides a semi-structured interview based on predetermined questions with the ability to probe if needed.

The initial phase involved this researcher contacting potential participants on the phone or in person to determine if they were willing and able to participate in the research. Once participants verbally committed to participating in the study, this researcher sent them an informed consent form. The informed consent explained the purpose, benefits, confidentiality, decision to quit and how the findings will be used in this research. The participants were required to provide their signature on the informed consent form before proceeding to the next phase of the study.

The second phase of the data collection process involved scheduling 60-minute sessions with each participant based on their individual availability. At the beginning of each session, this researcher reminded participants about the purpose of the research and that all responses would be kept confidential. This researcher asked all participants the same six questions to ascertain their thoughts, feelings, and experiences.

During the interviews, this researcher took notes to ensure the accuracy of recorded responses. The final stage of the data collection process involved participants verifying the accuracy of the data collected during the interviews. All participants were emailed a transcript of the interview along with a request to confirm the accuracy of the information within 5 days of receipt. If changes were requested by participants, a date and time were set up based on the availability of the respondent. Once the data were confirmed, the researcher sent a final email thanking each respondent for their participation in the study.

**Confidentiality.** Each participant was ensured that the confidentiality of the information they provided would not be disclosed in any case. To maintain anonymity, respondent names will not be collected and the results from the interviews were converted to a coded pseudonym. Additionally, the interviews were conducted only by this researcher to minimize the risk of confidential information being released.

**Data Storage.** The data were stored securely in the researcher's computer system. Triple copies will be made to ensure that the data is not lost in case of an error. The files were secured with a password known only to the researcher. Secure encryption of the password was done in the U.S.B. device to ensure proper protection. All these measures contributed to the participant's confidentiality and anonymity.

Dr. Radisha Brown

The Art of Storytelling

# Methodological Assumptions, Limitations, and Delimitations

## Methodological Assumptions

Effective and meaningful research should be conducted based on the research ethics, which need to be followed by the researcher throughout the entire process. The researcher must be aware of how to the ethical conduct research and when the conduct is considered as unethical.

All the participants in the research engaged in the systematic inquiry were fully informed. Only those respondents who were willing to participate were chosen. There are two types of consent; direct and substitute consent. Direct consent is the one which is obtained directly from the person who is participating. Substitute consent, on the other hand, is determined when the person is not capable of making a decision or is dependent on others (Nagy, Robert et. Al, 2005).

This study ensured the privacy and confidentiality of the data at every stage of the research and employed an open approach where the identity of the researcher, the purpose of the study, and

Dr. Radisha Brown

its methodology were known to all the people concerned. The data collected were kept safe by maintaining strict privacy checks on confidentiality. The researcher ensured that participants were informed, and consent given. The informed consent letter was given to the participants so that agreed mutual understanding took place between the researcher and the participants of the study.

# CHAPTER

# Data Processing and Analysis

"The qualitative data analysis technique can be regarded as the data enhancer technique" (Creswell, 2008, p. 65). This approach investigates the effect and diversity of the industry. The interview questions are based on the review of literature attained through secondary sources. The interview questions eliminated any technical words, unfamiliar words, and jargon (Burns & Grove, 2007; Creswell, 2008; O'Cathain, Murphy & Nicholl, 2007). In addition, ambiguous and imprecise concepts or words were avoided for the reduction of errors in responses to the questions (Johnson, Onwuegbuzie & Turner, 2007; Kumar, 2007).

Double- negative or double-barreled questions were avoided to reduce the chances of any confusion in the questions (Creswell, 2008). In the end, to formulate questions that are extremely reliable and valid, the survey did not "use questions that can create biases and are leading to the pre-formulated results" (Ketchen, Boyd & Bergh, 2008, pp. 649).

The data were analyzed by studying and organizing a large amount of data collected through secondary sources. The researcher sorted and organized data in alignment with the research questions

Dr. Radisha Brown

of the study, but was broadened through various sub-topics. The already available data were analyzed thoroughly and the research questions were kept as the main area of concern.

The participants' interviews were transcribed and copies of each merged into one Microsoft Word document for easy review and analysis. Interview responses were coded by the researcher to get the accurate, reliable, valid and relevant results. Common ideas, themes, expressions, and views were used as units for analysis. The data were organized into coherent relevant categories that summarized and brought meaning to the data.

This can be labor-intensive depending on the amount of data you have, but this is the crux of qualitative analysis (Taylor-Powell & Renner, 2003). This process consisted of identifying common themes and assigning an abbreviated code with letters or numbers that relate to the primary research topic. Additional themes found in the data were identified as a subcategory.

# Reliability and Validity

Validity and reliability are two important segments of quantitative research to approve and validate the quantitative research. Kirk and Miller (1986) identified "three types of reliability in quantitative research, which relate to: (1) producing the same results under same measurement conditions; (2) the stability of a measurement with respect to time; and (3) the similarity of measurements in a given time period" (p. 41-42). Earl (1989) has noted that the need to address the concept of reliability is met if the

The Art of Storytelling

researcher documents procedures in such a way that another researcher could easily conduct the same study again. Such requirements were met in this study by maintaining the chain of evidence.

Validity assesses whether the meaning and interpretation of an event are sound or whether a particular measure is an accurate reflection of intent. Researchers may check for validity in several ways. These include comparing the findings of one instrument with findings from other instruments and conducting joint observations or collaborative marking of the same tests. Checking validity could also include returning draft reports to respondents for accuracy checks, considering opposing explanations for the issue or question, and conducting multiple observations of the same event. The researcher can also enhance respondent validity by asking the participants to check their interpretations of the information provided or observed.

Another option to ensure validity when seeking data is to use a pre-designed measurement instrument, such as an existing instrument previously tested and found valid. Ensuring validity can be difficult and should be taken seriously and carefully and to show the impact of the collected data on the business.

The data were checked for validity by sending the interviewer's transcript back to each participant to verify that the responses were accurate. Utilizing such methods adds certainty that the data collected is valid and useful for planning and decision-making processes.

Dr. Radisha Brown

The Art of Storytelling

# RESULTS

This section first presents brief introductions to the participants. It summarizes demographics in tabular form, followed by expanded narrative descriptions that indicate pseudonyms (monikers) used to personalize individual participants and help readers distinguish them throughout the section.

The research first summarizes the emergent themes in tabular form, followed by individual sections that present evidence for each theme in narrative form.

Dr. Radisha Brown

The Art of Storytelling

# Brief Introductions to the Participants

Nine participants were interviewed, six males and three females. Table 1 shows participant demographics by age, gender, race, length of experience in years with their current employer and business sector.

Table 1    *Participants Demographics*

| M | A | Gend | Race | Servi | Sector |
|---|---|---|---|---|---|
| SW: Stable | 43 | M | African | 17 | Manufactu |
| AS: Reserved | 38 | M | African | 2.5 | Transporta |
| BC: Man with the | 48 | M | White | 0.5 | Finance |
| CC: Edgy | 45 | M | White | 7.5 | Mental |
| DB: Composed | 32 | M | White | 3.1 | Manufactu |
| BC2: Intrigued | 29 | M | White | 1.5 | Mental |
| SC: Ardent | 38 | F | African | 10 | Military |
| TC: Weary Clerk | 49 | F | White | 3.5 | Finance |
| SP: Committed | 45 | F | White | 3 | Mental |

Gender M = male. F = female. Service: Years in current position

The following section presents brief narrative introductions to the participants in alphabetical order. Based on demographic descriptions in Table 1 and characterizations gleaned from interviews, each participant was given a pseudonym (moniker) for ease of identification in the rest of the chapter. A common theme that emerged from the following introductions is frustration with their current working environment.

Dr. Radisha Brown

# AS: The Reserved Trucker

Participant AS is a 38-year-old African American male working as a truck driver in the transportation sector. AS generally enjoys working at working at this organization but said he is *frustrated* with its many changes.

At the start of the interview, AS sat back in the chair with his ankle on top of his knee and appeared to be interested in the topic of storytelling. His initial eye contact was good. However, over the course of the questions, he seemed to lose interest in discussion after the first two questions. He began to stare. This suggested that there was something about the role of storytelling in his professional life that made It somewhat antagonistic to or incompatible with him, but he did not provide many details.

When asked how his organization uses storytelling to communicate change, AS rolled his eyes but simply said that his company "tells a lot of stories." Yet he remained emotionally disconnected from the stories. As the interview progressed, AS repeatedly looked at his watch and began talking fast. Although he nodded throughout the interview, he had a scowl on his face.

AS is the Reserved Trucker.

# BC: The Money Man with the Halo

Participant BC is a 48-year-old White male working as an executive assistant in the financial services sector. BC has been with his current organization for just six months and said he is very *excited* about working at this new organization. Because he is a recent hire, BC is learning more about his organization every day. BC seemed genuinely interested throughout the interview.

The interview began with BC in an alert professional stance, sitting in the chair and pushing back on it with his shoulders. BC provided good eye contact while listening and speaking. He would look at the interviewer for a few seconds, glance away briefly and reinstate eye contact. BC was very definitive and emotionally engaged with the material although, again using the professional stance, provided answers with normal speech and only slight changes in his tone of voice.

When describing how his organization uses storytelling to communicate organizational change, BC smiled broadly. In his view, BC's organization does "an excellent job at communicating changes." BC did not look his watch during the interview and maintained a relaxed posture with his hands in his lap the entire time.

BC is the Money Man with the New Job Halo.

Dr. Radisha Brown

# BC2: The Intrigued Counselor

Participant BC2 is a 29-year-old White male working as a licensed Family and Marriage Counselor in the healthcare industry. BC2 was the youngest participant (Table 1). He has only been with his current organization for 1.5 years. He said he feels generally *frustrated* with his high-volume caseload.

Initially, BC2 seemed disinterested in the topic of storytelling but became increasingly engaged over the course of his interview.

When the interview began, he rocked back and forth slightly in his chair, his eyes wandering. However, when asked how his organization uses storytelling, he began to stare at the interviewer. His voice increased in volume and pitch. With increasing excitement, BC2 explained to himself how "employees don't like change and stories *could* help employees to be less resentful of change."

As he realized the impact of what he had just said, he began to nod in agreement with himself, surprised at his own revelation. Pulled into the positive influence of storytelling, BC2 smiled for the rest of the interview and remained engaged.

BC2 is the Intrigued Counselor.

# CC: The Edgy Counselor

Participant CC is a 45-year-old White male who grew up in a military family and who works as a licensed professional counselor in the healthcare industry. CC has been with his current organization for 7.5 years and recently changed roles. In his new role, CC works with a new program that is constantly changing. He said this creates *frustration*.

The interview began with the CC sitting with his back straight back in the chair with a scowl on his face. Throughout the interview, CC rubbed his hands together or sat with both his feet and his arms crossed, and generally made good eye contact but sometimes fixed the interviewer with a weird stare.

CC tended to provide clipped responses at a rapid rate of speech and/or with his voice slightly raised or flailed his arms when talking nervously. CC used a particularly harsh tone when recommending that organizations need to "Be real and don't tell *cute* stories that don't deal with the difficulties that do in reality arise." CC nodded excessively and looked at his watch several times throughout the interview.

CC is the Edgy Counselor.

Dr. Radisha Brown

# DB: The Composed Project Manager

Participant DB is a 32-year-old White male working as a project manager in the manufacturing sector. Employed with his current organization for precisely 3.1 years, DB tried to change roles but was "passed over" recently. DB said he is *frustrated* with his current role because of the routine changes in manufacturing.

The interview began with DB sitting with his back straight back in the chair with a big grin. Throughout the interview, he made good eye contact. He sat with his hands placed carefully in his lap. He responded carefully to each question and provided precise answers without elaboration in a normal speaking rate and tone of voice. However, he sometimes prefaced his remarks with the word "Well..."

DB was also reluctant to provide advice to leaders about storytelling as a tool for communicating organizational change. DB nodded his head in agreement during the interview and maintained a constant composure.

DB is the Composed Project Manager.

# SW: The Stable Manufacturing Manager

Participant SW is a 43-year-old African American male working as an account manager in the manufacturing sector. SW was not the oldest participant but had been with his current organization the longest, 17 years. SW said he is *frustrated* with his current role because "the company is undergoing a major shift as they are purchasing a large competitor".

Moreover, his organization recently laid off 1% of their workforce. SW routinely works very long hours. The interview began with SW sitting in the chair with a big smile across his face. Despite this, he rocked back and forth, touched his nose frequently and said he was nervous about the interview "with all of the stuff going on at this company".

Throughout the interview, SW maintained good eye contact and responded to each question very carefully. SW provided a particularly heartfelt response when discussing how storytelling can encourage employees to engage more fully with the company's mission but also cautioned that, "Older employees may be reluctant to buy-in because they have seen this type of strategy being used in the past."

SW is the Stable Manufacturing Manager.

Dr. Radisha Brown

# SC: The Ardent Support Specialist

Participant SC is a 38-year-old African American female working as a support specialist in the military services industry. SC has been with her organization for 10 years. She generally enjoys working at working at this organization but said she sometimes feels *frustrated* with the regularity of governmental changes.

When the interview began, SC sat with her back against the chair and her ankle resting on top of her knee. Throughout the interview, she provided good eye contact. SC got tearful when relating a story about how a fellow service member received the wrong medication due to a system issue. SC disclosed that this story taught her the importance of fully understanding all the rules before software is rolled out to healthcare providers.

When talking about how vital it is for all employees to understand the specific impacts of system change, she choked up. Her tone and voice changed again when discussing how useful storytelling is to communicate organizational changes because stories bring employees together and put everyone on one page. After the interview was completed, she sat soberly in the chair before leaving the room.

SC is the Ardent Support Specialist.

173 | P a g e

# SP: The Committed Counselor

Participant SP is a 45-year-old White female working as a licensed professional Mental Health Counselor in the healthcare industry. SP has been with her organization for 3 years. She loves working at her organization because she gets the opportunity to help an underserved population.

The interview began with SP sitting in a relaxed posture with a smile on her face. SP provided good eye contact during the interview. However, this changed when discussing an upsetting experience when her organization used storytelling to communicate organizational change. Slowing her speech and markedly lowering her voice, SP told how the story of a patient's suicide was used to poignantly reinforce the importance of documenting clinical interviews and filing them each day before leaving work.

She tearfully disclosed the tremendous impact that the suicide story had had on her daily process of writing and filing treatment notes as directed. She continued to repeat with vicarious dread, "I *never* want to have one of my patients commit suicide!" Her tone and voice changed again when discussing how useful storytelling is for communicating organizational changes because stories bring employees together. After her interview, SP immediately went to the restroom to wipe her face.

SP is the Committed Counselor.

Dr. Radisha Brown

# TC: The Weary Clerk

Participant TC is a 49-year-old White female working as a payroll clerk in the financial services sector. She has been with her organization for 3.5 years. She enjoys what she does but does not like a large number of recent organizational process changes.

Due to regular legislative changes, her company must constantly update insurance providers and employee benefit costs, which she admits, *"makes my job more difficult."* The interview began with TC sitting in a slumped position with her hands placed on top of her head. TC seemed to lose interest in the material after the first question. About 10 minutes into the interview, she began shaking her foot. Throughout the interview, she frowned almost continuously and made limited eye contact, staring instead at the floor or walls.

When disclosing her advice to leadership in the use of storytelling to communicate change, TC rolled her eyes and related, "Leaders need to be honest, thorough and clear when communicating with employees and they *must* understand the workload increase will have on employees." TC checked her watch throughout the interview.

TC is the Weary Clerk.

# Narrative Summaries of Participant Responses to Interview Questions

Table 2 summarizes themes that emerged from interviews. The overarching theme from the interviews was that storytelling is an agent of connection between a person and the point of a story. In Table 2, the phrase 'organizational storytelling' refers to organizational storytelling specifically *to communicate organizational change.*

Dr. Radisha Brown

Table 2 *Theme Summary*

| Topic | Emergent Theme |
| --- | --- |
| Employment | Overarching Theme: Most participants were frustrated with all the changes at work. |
| Entire Interview | Overarching Theme: Storytelling is an agent of connection between a person and the point of a story. |
| Explanations of Storytelling | Theme: Participants had different views of storytelling. Theme: Self-evident definitions<br>Theme: Complex definitions accompanied by the purpose of telling the story |
| Important Features of Storytelling | Theme: The story must be truthful and honest. Theme: The story's structure and characterization,<br>comprised of components that help listeners connect to the story to understand its message: the setting, personal traits of individuals in the story and vivid imagery |
| Experiences with their Organizational Storytelling | Theme: Storytelling has inherent appeal. Theme: Storytelling has subtle but persuasive power. |
| Feelings about Organizational Storytelling | Theme: Generally positive |
| Storytelling as a Tool to Engage Employees | Theme: Employees have unique views on engagement. Subtheme: Companies that communicate tend to engender greater engagement.<br>Theme: Storytelling does not guarantee increased engagement. It works for some employees some of the time. |
| Advice to Leadership about Organizational Storytelling | Theme: Storytelling must have obvious relevance to the change. |

The Art of Storytelling

The following sections describe participant responses by an interview question in narrative form. Each interview question provides the focus of the discussion. Comments are presented as evidence of the themes they were interpreted to represent.

# Interviewees' Explanations of Storytelling

The first interview question was, can you explain what storytelling is? The following comments suggest that participants explained storytelling with simple definitions or complex definitions accompanied by the purpose of storytelling. They show that the participants had different views of storytelling.

Responses fell into two broad categories or themes. One category was a basic description without reference to the purpose of storytelling. The most succinct description came from a White male who worked in manufacturing, the composed project manager DB: "Storytelling is a depiction of events, which is often improved and embellished." The other two participants who described storytelling without ascribing a purpose both included a timeframe.

The reserved African American trucker AS described storytelling as "the process of sharing information" in terms of "experiences, thoughts and ideas" that "can involve words and images". This is a rather obvious definition, especially because AS pointed out that storytelling "can involve words." However, AS's description of storytelling included a timeframe, specifically the "past, current, or future."

The only other participant to include a timeframe in her description was the ardent specialist SC, an African American woman with a military career, whose description of storytelling was strikingly similar to AS's description: "I think storytelling is the process in which thoughts and ideas are shared from one person to another." SC's reference to a timeframe, however, was distinctly different than AS's reference because she referred to the ancient past rather than the recent past, such as last year: "Historically, it [storytelling] was the process used by our ancestors to pass information from generation to generation." None of these descriptions referred to the emotional content of a story.

The other category was a description combined with the *purpose* of telling a story, which sometimes alluded to the emotional content of a story. The emergent themes included the role of a story as an agent of connection and that the participants tended to have different views of storytelling. Six of the nine participants fell into this category.

The three mental health counselors talked about the role of storytelling when working with clients in the therapeutic setting. The surprised counselor BC2, a White male mental health counselor who seemed to have stumbled upon his own revelations about the merits of storytelling during the interview, described storytelling as "talking about things that happen" but added that its purpose was "to help others understand a concept."

BC2 then elaborated with reference to the emotional context

of a story: "You tell stories to let other people know the depth, intensity, feelings to give a more rounded experience of the meaning that you are trying to portray." For BC2, the purpose of storytelling is to explain or convey.

The edgy counselor CC, who grew up as a military family, described storytelling as "a way to tell entertaining and fascinating ideas with characters, settings, which often have a moral or lesson that inspires people." For CC, the purpose of storytelling is to inspire.

These two counselors' responses were concise and thorough descriptions that additionally articulated the purpose of storytelling. One might suspect that being a counselor influenced these responses because storytelling, told by both counselors and clients, is a potent therapeutic tool. This researcher was pleasantly surprised that some participants had such clear ideas about the role of storytelling. Again, though, counseling is a career in which storytelling may play a larger part than, for example, accounts payable in a manufacturing plant.

These comments also imply that one tells stories to communicate some larger meaning or lesson. Stories in the context of this study were those used to communicate larger meanings. But not all stories are told for that lofty purpose.

The committed counselor SP is also a White mental health counselor, but her view of storytelling was quite different from her colleagues. She distinguished stories from the professional literature: "I think storytelling is to tell something to someone else that is either true or not true.

It is a way to convey information instead of literature based."

Dr. Radisha Brown

Popular and professional literature on a topic both convey information. But SP appears to be thinking about the professional literature, suggesting that she sees a very clear distinction between the formality of technical reports and a nice friendly story told to make a point. Later in the interview, SP would state flatly that, "Literature are boring."

The role of storytelling with clients in therapeutic settings differs from the perspective of a company telling a story to engage employees in the company mission, persuade them to embrace [the reason for] a policy change, or soften the blow of an unpopular organizational change. For the stable manufacturing manager SW, an African American male with long-term experience in the manufacturing sector, "Storytelling is the use of personal or connected experiences that help to motivate individuals to laugh or find a connection with the story being told." For SW, the purpose of storytelling was also to "connect" individuals to the point of the story".

For the weary clerk TC, a White female working in the financial sector, the purpose of storytelling is also to connect. But her comments suggest that she was thinking about external connections, such as linking a company's product with its customers, rather than storytelling as an agent of connection between a person and the point of a story. Here is how she framed her answer to the question; can you explain what storytelling is? "Corporate storytelling is how the most successful companies use marketing and communications to move their businesses ahead."

The Art of Storytelling

In contrast to TC, the other participants tended to think about storytelling in terms of communicating internally with employees. However, TC's somewhat nebulous reference to "communications to move their businesses ahead" may or may not refer to internal storytelling to communicate with employees.

By far the most articulate description and stated purpose of storytelling came from the money man with the new job halo BC. Even though BC is a White male in the financial sector, his description reads like something one might expect from one of the mental health counselors in the study. This is because, as discussed above, counselors are, presumably, frequently called upon to penetrate client stories for deeper meanings in the interest of developing therapy: "Stories can be used to study often unstated and perhaps unconscious codes for resolving conflicts, approaching decision-making, determining perceptions of positive and negative organizational forces, guiding role behavior, and the like. Stories are also defined, prior research is described, and the advantages and disadvantages of using this technique." This is a deep and thoughtful view of storytelling. It also seems more likely to have come from one of the mental health counselor interviewees because it refers to the role of prior research, but because the reference is fleeting, it is unclear to what research BC referred.

The above articulations of the definition and purpose of storytelling argue that the participants tended to have different views of storytelling. The next section, which presents the features that are the most important to storytelling, tends to confirm that

Dr. Radisha Brown

interpretation of different views of storytelling.

# Important Features of Storytelling

For the second interview question, participants were asked to describe what they believe to be the important features of storytelling. The following comments suggest that two themes emerged. One theme was that a story must be truthful and honest. The other theme, the story's structure and characterization, were comprised of key components that helped listeners connect to the story so that they understand its message: describing the setting and personality traits of individuals in the story and creating vivid imagery. Similar to participants' explanations of storytelling (previous section), the story's important features depicted storytelling as an agent of connection between a person and the point of a story.

Several participants underscored the theme of truth and honesty. TC, the weary clerk, said bluntly, but without elaboration: "Important features should include honesty and details." TC may be describing the 'story' behind a successful marketing campaign. The intrigued counselor BC2, the youngest participant at age 29 years, also spoke of truth, "I believe that storytelling...depends on if you are telling something that is true or false," reiterating that "it is important that the information is truthful." Like TC, BC2 also included "details" as another important feature of a story.

The composed project manager DB put it this way: "Well, important features of storytelling include stories that are interesting, relevant, and credible." The reserved trucker AS said the same thing

The Art of Storytelling

more glibly: "I also believe that storytelling provides a measure of truth that individuals can relate to."

Another set of responses pertained to the story's structure and characterization rather than its inherent veracity. Some of the comments about structure were brief. CC, the edgy counselor, emphasized that important features included the "setting...where the story takes place and how that sets the mood for the moral or helps to illustrate the nature of the characters."

AS, the reserved trucker who never quite warmed to the topic, also talked about structure: "I believe that storytelling is, uh, involves people describing specifics such as when, where an event took place." His perspective runs along the lines of structuring a story by the classic who, what, when, where and why of a story we are taught in middle school English class.

In contrast to BC's elaborated response to the definition and purpose of storytelling, the money man with the new job halo had severely truncated views of the important features of storytelling: "Identification. Conflict resolution. Guided role behavior. Process flow". Conflict resolution is a technical way to think about everyday problems at work and raised questions about BC's education and background, belied by his current position as an executive assistant. CC, the edgy counselor, also provided a curt list of storytelling's important features: "Characters: Antagonists. Protagonist." After a pause, CC added, "Three-dimensional characters, that is, ones with the depth of personality, faults, more than one personality trait exemplified..." and his voice trailed off.

Dr. Radisha Brown

SC, the ardent specialist who choked up when relating the story about a fellow service member who received the wrong medication due to a system issue, used the word structure: "I think that storytelling should include a structured description of events, people, and places. I believe that the story should have a central theme, relatable characters that [sic] have some sort of struggle between good and evil. It [storytelling] should be [used to] evoke an emotional response so that the listener feels *connected* to the outcome."

The intrigued counselor BC2 also implied the connection between the story and listeners, although he thought that the important feature of storytelling is to see the story mentally: "I want to get an image of the concept of what you are talking about." Thinking about the reception to a story, he added, "Too much information might be overkill.

Emphasis and use of different tones are important to keep the audience's attention." It is a powerful story indeed that can leave the listener with an image of a concept.

SP, the committed counselor who got so emotional when telling the suicide story, also named imagery as an important feature of storytelling: "I think that it is important to concentrate on the imagery when telling a story. It is important [for the story] to have historical or moral relevance." At first, perhaps thinking of the patient who committed suicide, SP said the important feature was to be germane to loved ones: "It should be relevant and contribute to each family in that generation." Then she switched gears and spoke of staff members: "Storytelling must motivate and inform employees what they need to do because they [need to] understand why. Things need to make sense to use because the importance needs to be conveyed. It should give options such as, what if we did it like this or that, and the consequences for each action. The before and after a change should be communicated." SP's easily-triggered emotionality expressed itself in the above passage, which is not easy to understand the first time it is read, as if her words rushed forward, refusing to form whole sentences.

SW, the stable manager with so much manufacturing experience under his belt, went into detail as if he had given storytelling a lot of thought.

> *The important features of storytelling are the introduction, development of the climactic situation, and ending. The listener must understand who or what the basis of the story is. The listener must be able to identify when the story has reached a climactic development. To create a purposeful connection, this portion of the story must resonate with the listener. Once this has been achieved, the listener is engaged and there is a strong possibility the ending will aid in setting the stage for the desired change needed.*

The above comments show that two themes emerged from consideration of the important features of a story. One theme was that a story is truthful and honest. The other theme, the story's structure and characterization, were comprised of components that helped the listeners connect to the story so that they understand its message: the setting, the personal traits of individuals in the story and vivid imagery. That is, the story's most important features depict it as an agent of connection between a person and the point of a story.

Dr. Radisha Brown

# Experience with Corporate Storytelling to Communicate Organizational Change

For the third interview question, participants were asked to discuss their experiences with their organizations using storytelling to communicate organizational change. The theme that emerged from these conversations was the inherent appeal of storytelling along with its subtle, but persuasive power. Not all the participants, however, succumbed to its power at this point in the interview, as the following comments reveal.

By this point in the interviews, several participants seemed to embrace the idea of storytelling because they started telling stories themselves. This underscores the inherent appeal of storytelling along with its subtle powers of persuasion. As the participants' stories reveal, storytelling can also exert significant influence when used to communicate important professional policies, but also the dismal and dire consequences of failure.

BC2, the intrigued counselor, summarized the following story:

> I have not had my organization use stories to communicate changes. There is a chance that my previous leaders have used storytelling, but they may have been subtle that I don't remember them. However, I can think of stories that could have been useful for the leaders to use to communicate change. As an example, there was a situation with another counselor where she was inappropriate with a client. This was a serious situation that caused the loss of her license and job. The leaders could have used this story as a tool to communicate the importance of therapists asking for help and appropriately working with clients.

SP, the committed counselor, recalled her chilling suicide story.

> *I remember when, during training, my boss told me of a story of a patient committing suicide and the counselor had not placed any treatment notes in the chart. It conveyed the importance of treatment notes being [on] the chart for the investigative purposes. From the story, I clearly understood why putting treatment notes in the chart was [so important]. Before that time, in other jobs, we were simply told via lecture to do things and we were not told why. In this situation, it helped me to understand why I needed to put treatment notes in the charts every day before I leave each day.*

SC, the ardent specialist, revealed that the military uses storytelling often and effectively.

> *During my time working for the Department of Defense, stories are routinely discussed to inspire change within the organization. I remember the organization was rolling out a new software to track medications for service members. We were told a story of a service member whose file was set up incorrectly, so he received a medication that he was allergic to. It was a nightmare because he was a single dad with two young children. The medication caused severe damage and the service member was hospitalized for several days. Thankfully, he made a great recovery, but that story reinforced the importance of the software being set up correctly.*

CC, the edgy counselor, did not share a specific story but rather confirmed SC's observation about the large role of storytelling by the military: "I grew up in the military. In the military, there are many stories that are told about wars, special units or battalions, that are taught to the troops, which convey shared qualities and values. I grew up listening to these stories and hearing about them." One might suspect that, despite his general unease during the interview, the combination of CC's upbringing and career choice of counseling together created his distinct ideas about storytelling.

Dr. Radisha Brown

DB, the composed project manager, told part of a story.

> *Well, I have seen mixed results. Some leaders are better storytellers than others. In fact, I believe that the ability to use storytelling effectively can really enhance a leader's success. The best example I've seen was a VP of Customer Service telling a call center group stories about bad experiences at McDonald's and good experiences at Chick-Fil-A. It really underscored the importance of good service in terms everyone could understand.*

The reserved trucker AS was refreshingly but uncharacteristically forthcoming in response to this topic, revealing that he would prefer the use of storytelling as a tool of communication if it were available:

> *My experience has been limited because my [transportation] company typically uses PowerPoint presentations and videos to communicate changes. Occasionally, we may have a training coach describe his personal experience with commercial driving and how the industry has tremendously changed. Unfortunately, they really don't spend a lot of time telling stories when I think there are a lot of stories to share because I learn the most when I hear stories.*

Two participants skillfully evaded the question. BC, the money man with the new job halo, had an expectedly glowing response without answering the question: "Currently our company does an excellent job of communicating in a very open weekly staff meeting using technology on Mondays about the health of the business to personal accomplishments and opportunities." Perhaps he can be forgiven for essentially evading the question, which may reflect the halo effect of a delightful new job with a fresh new company. Nonetheless, whether his company had used storytelling as a communication tool is unclear.

With unexpected vigor, the weary clerk TC also made glowing remarks about her company. Like BC, she did not answer the question

The Art of Storytelling

directly. "Our company has really improved the way in which it communicates to employees. Employees are encouraged to highlight issues during the weekly staff meetings and to discuss ways in which the company can improve." She does not mention storytelling, so it is unclear if TC has exposure to it or whether her company used storytelling as a communication tool.

SW, the stable manufacturing manager, simply offered that, "Storytelling is used in organizations quite often to engage the listeners to rally behind the company's mission or goal." Uncharacteristically, he did not elaborate. However, later in the interview, he would reveal a likely reason for his reticence.

The above commentary argues that recollections of organizational storytelling as a tool to communicate change aptly illustrated the inherent appeal of storytelling, given that several, but not all, participants began sharing stories. Indicative of the subtle but persuasive power of storytelling, their stories also illustrated that simply recollecting stories reveals that storytelling is an agent of connection between a person and the point of a story.

# Feelings about Storytelling to Communicate Change

The above discussion about participant experiences with organizational storytelling as a tool to communicate change was designed to accomplish two things: glean information, as well as gently warm participants up to the next interview question, the topic of this section.

Dr. Radisha Brown

This interview question asked them to describe their feelings and responses to organizational storytelling as a tool to communicate change. Feelings were generally expressed with positive adjectives (Table 3). The quality and nature of the adjectives revealed a theme of strong advocacy of storytelling as an effective communication tool, underscored by subtler implications that it serves as an agent of connection between a person and the point of a story.

Table 3

*Feelings Described as Positive Adjectives about Organizations using Storytelling to Communicate Change*

| Topic | Positive Adjectives |
|---|---|
| Feelings about Corporate Storytelling to Communicate organizational Change | Emotional personal connection More personable <br> Humanizing Valid <br> Appropriate <br> Motivational <br> Connect me to the change emotionally Useful <br> Propaganda but it feels good <br> Stories made me feel proud and have a sense of duty <br> Effective <br> Positive <br> Very powerful when used by a charismatic leader <br> Greater understanding of the impact of change |

Nonetheless, this section begins with comments that were generally negative reflections as a counterpoint. The intrigued counselor and weary clerk addressed the emotional impact of impending or unavoidable change on employees, creating a vivid image of employee feelings when a company announces the change. BC2: "Employees typically don't like change and if there is a lot of change, employees will be resentful and frustrated with the

The Art of Storytelling

changes." Reiterating her personal theme of the lack of corporate candor, TC became almost petulant in her frustration at the lack of corporate honesty in the face of organizational change:

> *I desire that organizations would be clear and honest with their employees. During my career, I found that organizations try to get employees to accept changes without full explanations and it is difficult as an employee to accept changes just because someone has decided that things need to be changed. I believe it is important for employers to be honest and upfront with employees.*

TC does not mention storytelling directly nor does she describe her feelings about any stories she has been told in the context of communicating organizational change. But she does not have to – does not have to use words, that is. Her body language clearly informed the interviewer that the corporate stories she has heard consistently lacked veracity, leading to her irrepressible frustration.

On the lighter side, two participants said that stories in the context of change helped them make an emotional connection to impending change, further implicating storytelling as an agent of connection between a person and the point of a story. Reserved trucker AS was actually forthcoming: "I think that storytelling provides more of an emotional personal connection that reinforces the information given. It, uh, also when you hear stories, it is more personable [personal] and you can relate better to the information. I also believe that it humanizes the person and the company." The intrigued counselor BC2 also thought stories helped him relate to the information better: "If the organization could use stories and things to connect [me to] the change emotionally, I would have been more receptive to the changes."

Their comments raise a question. As relatively young men, was age related to AS and BC2's feelings that their company was responsible, or played a role, in their emotions about the job? Just recently have corporations felt pressure to develop some level of "corporate conscience" and take some responsibility for promoting an emotionally happy and nurturing environment for employees. Such a thing was unheard of two decades ago. With respect to the main aim of the current research, what role might future storytelling play in creating kinder, gentler corporations?

CC, the edgy counselor, clearly articulated his emotional response to storytelling: "Well, in the military, it [storytelling] is a bit like propaganda, but it feels good. I always liked watching war movies and hearing about the stories, made me feel proud and have a sense of duty." For CC, cantankerous though he may have been, storytelling created a sense of pride in his country. No one else mentioned stories as eliciting pride. Pride is a motivating force. Committed counselor SP pointed out that her experience with the suicide story "motivated me to do what I needed to do."

The rest of the participants spoke in terms of the positive influence of storytelling on communicating change by citing adjectives (italicized below for ease of recognition), which were different forms of feelings than emotional connections. BC, the money man with the new job halo, said storytelling "allows the organization to help guide behaviors and clearly define desired results and outcome.

The Art of Storytelling

193 | P a g e

I believe that it's [storytelling] a *valid* form of communicating change." BC2 said, "I think that organizations use storytelling in the appropriate context to *motivate* change…. I think that storytelling is a *useful* way to communicate changes." Composed manager DB allowed that "Storytelling is *effective,* and I view it as a *positive element* of change management." Ardent specialist SC concurred: "I feel that storytelling is a *useful* tool to communicate change. It helps everyone to understand the wider impact of the change. It [storytelling] creates a focal point for individuals to gain a greater understanding of the impact of the change."

Taking a slightly different tack, the always-thoughtful stable manager SW directed his comments to the storyteller: "Depending upon the speaker, storytelling can be an *effective* method [to engage the listeners to rally behind company's mission or goal]. This method is *very powerful* when being used by a leader who possesses charismatic qualities."

The above feelings about storytelling to communicate company change were generally expressed with positive adjectives. The emergent theme was one of strong advocacy of storytelling as an effective communication tool. It was underscored by subtler implications that storytelling serves as an agent of connection between a person and the point of a story.

Dr. Radisha Brown

# Storytelling as a Tool to Engage Employees

As an agent of connection between a person and the point of a story, does storytelling have enough influence to affect engagement? Following questions about their experiences and feelings, participants were then asked to talk about their perspectives on the ability of storytelling to encourage full engagement from employees. This question elicited less consensus among the participants than any other point of discussion during the interviews.

The emergent themes were that employees probably have unique views of engagement and, whereas companies that communicate tend to engender greater engagement, storytelling was no guarantee of increasing engagement. The idea that employees probably have unique views of engagement was of interest to this researcher, especially upon noting that none of the participants attempted to define what they meant by engaged employees; the implication is that employee engagement is a known commodity that does not require description.

DB, the composed project manager, made an excellent point: "Storytelling is really a monologue, not a dialogue, so it does not engage the employees in terms of a conversation. However, if a story is interesting, you are far more likely to get someone's attention and have them engaged in listening." Admittedly, communicating company change is less often a conversation than being informed of the change, certainly from the perspective of front-line staff

The Art of Storytelling

members. Employees are not often a part of creating the change, just implementing it. Upper management creates the change.

The reserved trucker and intrigued counselor both talked about storytelling as a unifying influence. In their own way, each pointed out that every employee has a different perspective on what constitutes an engagement with their job; mere storytelling may not be enough. Here is how reserved trucker AS put it:

> *I believe that it [storytelling] does encourage some employees to fully engage. However, action speaks louder than words, so a company must support their words in action and deeds. I also think that some people have preconceived notions and no matter how much effort a company puts into engaging them, it will not work."*

Here is how the intrigued counselor BC2 put it, adding an important suggestion at the end on how companies may employ storytelling more effectively:

> *I agree that it [storytelling] can encourage engagement but understand that some people only think about themselves, so they will not be receptive to change. Some people will respond in the same matter despite what process [is] being used to communicate the change. Changes are difficult, so the stories need to be repeated.*

The money man with the new job halo, BC, also referred to each employee's unique perspective on engagement but focused on a positive outcome, implying that storytelling is a good platform. BC also refers to understandable emotional responses among employees confronted with change but who are expected to remain engaged.

> *I believe that people operate from a different place when an organization is transparent both with positive and negative organizational forces. Storytelling is one way of*

Dr. Radisha Brown

*forcing out fear and allowing people to engage in a controlled and positive place. I feel that employees operate from a different place if you give them a platform to engage.*

This topic elicited a concrete response from TC, the weary clerk, who conceptualized the role of storytelling in promoting engagement as creating a common ground from which to move forth.

*People are different in that they have different beliefs in which they use to make decisions. Storytelling is a way of setting the stage so that everyone starts from a singular basis. Storytelling helps to balance out the inequities that inherently exist in an organization. It creates a common ground.*

Both ardent specialist SC and committed counselor SP echoed the weary clerk's comments that storytelling encourages engagement by establishing a common ground. SC referred to common ground with a metaphor and added a thought about an emotional dimension - resistance - that can discourage engagement: "I think that storytelling brings employees together and helps everyone to be on one page. Storytelling helps to gain the acceptance of understanding of employees to prevent resistance.

Storytelling helps employees to feel engaged in the process." SP augmented her reference to common ground by claiming that another emotional dimension that can discourage engagement, tuning out, can be offset by relevant information: "Storytelling brings employees together on the certain level. It engages them at a given time so that they are less likely to tune out information. It makes the information relevant. I believe that it keeps people engaged in being told information."

Edgy counselor CC, perhaps as a function of his militaristic

The Art of Storytelling

197 | P a g e

background, seemed to scoff at the notion that the company is responsible for promoting employee engagement, storytelling notwithstanding. He bluntly argued that "Everyone should be involved [i.e., engaged]." But he adds a company role, though he barely implies that storytelling is a good mechanism for encouraging employee engagement: "Everyone needs to have the basic values and principles of the organization inculcated and internalized."

Finally, SW, the stable manufacturing manager with vast experience, had a cautionary tale to tell. He believes that storytelling does not encourage engagement for everybody, warning that storytelling "works effectively on newer employees to an organization. Older employees may be reluctant to 'buy-in' because they have seen this type of strategy being used earlier in his or her career." SW's implication - that storytelling can be used negatively or dishonestly by the company - may be biographic in nature. It is mildly reminiscent of TC's frustration with the lack of corporate candor.

The above commentary suggested that storytelling does not have a universal influence on employee engagement although it works for some employees some of the time. To round out the discussions, the final question pertained to advice for leadership.

Dr. Radisha Brown

# Advice to Leaders about Using Storytelling to Communicate Organizational Change

There is great satisfaction in Monday morning quarterbacking, a colloquialism for knowing all the answers. The final interview question indulged the participants by asking if they have any advice for leadership regarding the use of storytelling to communicate organizational change. On the tail of the most equivocal topic (above, storytelling and engagement), the theme that emerged from responses to this question was the most unequivocal: relevance.

DB, the composed project manager, was reluctant to provide advice to leaders about storytelling as a tool for communicating organizational change. Yet he did not waste words. His mild but concise advice: "Keep it interesting, relevant, and credible." In snappish contrast, edgy counselor CC virtually growled out his advice to keep the stories relevant: "Be real. Don't tell *cute* stories, that don't deal with the difficulties that do in reality arise."

Ardent specialist SC was also very clear in referencing relevance in her advice:

> I would recommend that the leaders use relevant stories that accurately depict the need for the change. Storytelling is an entry point and should be backed up with action on the organization. Finally, leaders should understand that some people just hear the story and some people are able to translate them into a picture. Therefore, it is important to understand that everyone gains something different from the stories. No one-story-fits-all approach!

The Art of Storytelling

SC added an excellent point that not everyone 'hears' the same story. In fact, each employee may well hear a different story. This echoes BC2's earlier advice: "Changes are difficult, so the stories need to be repeated."

In response to questions about advice he would give leadership, BC2 reiterated the idea of repeated exposure:

> *I would recommend that if you are going to use storytelling, make sure that you use multiple stories so that everyone that you are talking to can relate because everyone will not relate to the same story. Be dedicated to the cause. Demonstrate through the story how things might benefit those that [sic] will be affected by changes.*

Committed counselor SP talked about relevance this way: "I would say that employees tend to do things when they can generalize relevance. Using storytelling keeps the material interesting and hopefully brings about compliance." Then she reiterated her personal theme about the professional literature: "Literatures are boring, and people tend not to retain the information." This, then, is one of the many arguments put forth by the participants that storytelling is an effective corporate communication tool because it is as an agent of connection between a person and the point of a story.

Reserved trucker AS made a good point. His indirect reference to relevance was embedded in his implication that there is a crucial difference between the effective use of storytelling and a company simply "telling stories".

Telling stories raises often justifiable suspicion among employees.

> *I would recommend that the stories be current and relate*

Dr. Radisha Brown

> *to the audience. I want to hear stories about someone that I can relate to - not someone that [sic] does not understand what I do. I would recommend that the leader provides truthful information and not something that they made up to manipulate the workers. Employees know when they are being lied to.*

Weary clerk TC again mentioned her personal theme of the lack of corporate candor in addressing the question of advice to leadership: "Leaders need to be honest, thorough and clear and understand the increased workload that they are placing on their employees.

The stories need to be connected to the organizational change and the employees. It is important to emotionally engage employees with stories if you want to reduce employee resistance." TC mentioned honesty five different times, that is, in five out of the six interview questions.

The always-thoughtful stable manufacturing manager SW again came up with a unique perspective. One might feel the urge to secure SW's services in consulting with companies on the effective use of storytelling. His advice harkens back to DB'S point, earlier in the interview, that storytelling is a monologue rather than dialogue:

> *If you are going to use this strategy [of storytelling], you must be consistent throughout the change process. The employees are looking for leadership during this time. The management must make sure change does not disrupt daily operations. Effective storytelling can be used to bridge tough conversations and communicate throughout all levels of the organization.*

The advice to leadership, from the man with the new job halo, is not entirely clear: "Storytelling should be used to encourage conversation to organically grow through the organization." What BC meant by 'organically' or 'organically grow through the organization'

The Art of Storytelling

is uncertain, although it might be another way of expressing the colloquial term for inter-personal communication, the grapevine.

The Art of Storytelling

# Summary

Several major themes emerged from the interviews (Table 2). Two overarching themes emerged throughout the narratives, which should be taken into consideration when reading the other interpretations. One overarching theme corresponded to all but two of the participants themselves, that of frustration with their current job.

The other overarching theme, which corresponded to all the participants, was that storytelling is an agent of connection between a person and the point of a story. Remaining themes emerged from each of the six interview questions.

The first question asked participants to describe their personal explanations of storytelling and revealed three themes. Their descriptions suggested that each participant had their unique view of storytelling, which fell into the themes of self-evident definitions and the theme of complex definitions accompanied by the purpose of telling the story.

The second question asked participants to describe the important features of storytelling and revealed two themes. One, the story must be truthful and honest. Two, the story's structure and characterization ought to include components that helped the

Dr. Radisha Brown

204 | P a g e

listeners connect to the story and understand its message. Components included the setting, the personal traits of individuals in the story and vivid imagery.

The third question asked participants to describe their experiences with organizational storytelling used in the context of communicating organizational changes to staff members. Two themes emerged. In this context, storytelling has inherent appeal and subtle but persuasive power.

On the heels of questions about experiences, the fourth question asked participants to describe their feelings about organizational storytelling used in the context of communicating organizational changes to staff members. The theme was that storytelling was an effective tool.

The fifth question asked participants to describe their experiences with storytelling as a tool to engage employees. Two themes, one with a subtheme, emerged. The theme that employees tended to have unique views of engagement was underscored by the subtheme of companies that communicate tend to engender greater engagement. The second theme was that storytelling does not guarantee an increase in engagement, only working for some employees some of the time.

The sixth question asked participants for their advice to leadership about how to employ storytelling when communicating organizational change. The single theme was unequivocal: Storytelling must have obvious relevance to the change.

The Art of Storytelling

# CHAPTER FIVE: SUMMARY AND CONCLUSIONS

Today's business environment requires companies to routinely change to remain competitive. The globalization and technological evolution force companies to improve their business practices to survive. The changes may be minor, for instance, installation of new software. But the changes are often major, such as revamping an overall marketing strategy. Many people consider reorganization as the inability to perform effectively and getting things done due to continuous change. For them, this process shifts the organization from product development and customer support.

After the relaxation in global trade barriers, new competitors emerged, and new substitute products became available quickly. Following this trend, companies take advantage of new opportunities and perceived competitive advantage. Therefore, it is better to establish a corporate culture that enables companies to promote the organizational change.

Visionary organizations respond to factors that can bring change intelligently. Economic conditions, political changes, varying consumer demands, management policy and employment levels are always easy to brush aside the steady organizations. At the same

Dr. Radisha Brown

time, successful organizations keep their basic philosophy intact, because if an organization must meet the challenges of a changing world, it must be prepared to change everything about itself except (its basic) beliefs as it moves through corporate life; the only sacred cow in an organization should be its basic philosophy of doing business.

At present, the majority of the organizations across the globe function under escalating demands for change. The market has drastically changed due to high competition, technological advancement, increased customer demands and globalization. This rapidity of change requires organizations to change their organizational behavior and policies so that they can effectively become accustomed to market shifts.

The fast-paced changes in development programs and projects usually result in disappointing results. For any organization to effectively manage change, the change in competency should increase. Change competency is defined as the capability of an organization to effectively manage the changes in the environment and to be competent enough to become part of this continuous process.

Organizational change is referred to a process in which an organization optimizes its performance as it targets to acquire an idealistic position in the market. From a subjective point of view, organizational change takes place as a response to turbulent business environments or as a reaction to crisis situations. A more proactive perspective of organizational change is change prompted by senior management. This organizational change is particularly evident in organizations that experience shifts in senior management. The main causes of organizational change can be determined in the light of the following theories: dialectical theory, life-cycle theory, and teleological theory.

According to the teleological viewpoint, organizational change is an effort to attain an ideal state in the market through a continuous process of planning, execution, assessment, and reformation. The life-cycle theory argues that an organization is a body whose functions typically depend upon the external environment; various cycles are involved in the phases of birth, growth, maturation, and declination. The dialectical theory assumes that an organization, to a certain extent, is like a multicultural society with contrasting principals. In the context of this theory, organizational change is evident when one force dominates over others.

The leadership management of an organization plays a significant role in managing turbulent environments at the time of the change process. The fundamental responsibility of leadership management is to convey the goals and vision according to the change. Employees generally can work harder due to increases in pressure, but to enhance the effectiveness of their work, it is imperative to explain to them why they are required to do so and the aims and objectives behind it. It is important for the person in charge to carry through with the change and remain patient because positive outcomes do not come at once.

Dr. Radisha Brown

In recent times, there has been a significant increase in the interest of the leadership management regarding the influence a culture has on the ability to learn and change. Understanding planned and development change or organizational learning is not possible without taking into consideration culture as a fundamental source of resistance to change. The culture has a huge impact on the process of change; culture wins the race against strategy every time.

This is because a modified strategy will not result in the required change unless the effective changes in culture are made accordingly. The leadership management cannot simply execute organizational changes only by the means of systems and structures. They need to focus on their current organizational culture and determine whether their existing culture is adaptive to change. If not, they need to form a new and stronger basis for unity. It is important for organizations to be aware of their culture, holistic nature and the way in which their employees affect each other.

Facilitating change in an organization is a very difficult process, especially when the stakeholders view the change as unnecessary. When individuals are "confronted by change, people go through a time of transition that is rarely easy." During change, leaders must be resilient. Courage is a required characteristic. Leadership requires courage because you are trying to do things you think are right, with no guaranteed results.

Resistance is the process by which employees oppose change. Resistance is so common and so destructive to efforts to implement change that the quest to understand its forms is the

The Art of Storytelling

bedrock to managing change successfully. Resistance is a natural occurrence. Employees resist change because they want things to stay the same and they believe that this change will be bad for them. well as develop a plan that anticipates resistance but has a way to overcome it.

In summary, to lead change effectively, you must recognize that the phenomenon of change does not need managing as much as do the people involved with it. It is important that leaders are equipped with the skills needed to effectively guide subordinates through organizational change. Storytelling is one of the skills that leaders can employ during organizational change.

Motivation may come from the ambitions of the organization or the pain that it is going through because of the internal or external factors that require the organization to change. Different organizations at a different point in time need to have different changes for the organization to keep up with the environment and to keep the competitive edge.

The change of direction by the company is due to three main reasons. First, the reason could be that management wants or needs to spend less money. Second, the organization wants to make more money out of the present resources. Third, it may be the combination of both. Bringing about change is not easy.

Organizational change management is the concept which is dedicated to the management of the ideas and procedures in an orderly and effective way. The process of change management is not an easy procedure to implement. Many organizations know they

Dr. Radisha Brown

need change management, and they know that they need it to achieve set targets, but they don't exactly know what they want it for.

If we see it in a broader sense, change management involves two areas, one of which is the strategic alignment and the other is the organizational alignment.

Organizational alignment deals with communication of the expectations, messages and the priorities that are thought to be achieved out of the maximum levels of change management. The challenge to change management becomes tactical, as it shifts towards being a project or program level change management.

There are four main reasons why people resist change: 1) they did not know; 2) they were not able to; 3) they were not involved; 4) they are not willing to. Organizations are successful when their people start to think and act differently and are open to all the changes that might come their way. The highest levels of performance will result in the habit of 'no new change' and will hinder their path to the achievement of goals. In other words, change management is all about the dimensions of processes, people, and the technology.

This dissertation concludes that there is a strong relationship between storytelling and effective organizational change because the organizational commitment and resilience are directly proportional to each other. The literature review communicated that in complex settings, sense-making is facilitated through storytelling and stories.

The Art of Storytelling

Resilience and commitment are both very important at organizational as well as individual levels because they are the main sources for implementing organizational change. If people in an organization exhibit a higher degree of commitment to, and resiliency towards, their organization, then there is a greater probability of successful organizational change.

The members of an organization should follow a core ideology, which is based on teamwork and loyalty, through which they can achieve the long-term growth for their organization and lead to successful competitiveness in the future. The successful companies of the world always blend their business strategies with their core business purposes and values.

Moreover, they keep on changing their business operations and strategies so that they can compete in a changing world. Organizational change is also very important for the employees as well as for the sustainable development of the organization. It is essential for the managers and leaders to identify the core areas and aspects where change can be implemented in the organization through different channels. It is an important job of the leaders and managers to investigate different matters of the organization and build some common values, which they can then establish throughout the organization for success.

Communication is the glue that binds members, subunits, and organizations. The challenge is to adopt perspectives that include more communication and reduce the complexity of understanding the process message, which produces the greatest practical value in

Dr. Radisha Brown

managing the problems related to communication.

Organizational communication has two dominant interests: the skills that make them more efficient in communication among individuals in their work, and the factors that characterize the communication efficiency in the system. There are four major approaches to understanding organizational communication: communication as a) transfer of information, b) transactional process, c) strategic control, and d) balance between creativity and constraint. In the end, I propose a fifth way judged more complete: the organizational model based on the use of storytelling to communicate change.

Today, with the ease of sharing content on the internet, individuals have many opportunities and platforms to tell these stories in the digital environment. But there is a difference between children's stories and business stories. A well-told story can truly convey what happened to that organization, from its beginning to its development during all the years of existence. This is how organizations begin to create more connection with the audience and go on to develop commercial relationships. With the advent of the use of this information via transmedia, or through various communication channels and media, the intelligence in this storytelling and the way it is involved in these channels will make a difference over competitors.

It is imperative for organizations to understand that the human resources of the organization play an integral role in achieving the success of the change process. The employees are key to the

The Art of Storytelling

213 | P a g e

successful implementation of a change program. Therefore, it is important for organizations to successfully communicate the change plan to its employees before undertaking any action because, without the contribution of the employees, the change plan can never achieve its true goal.

Stories can play a great role in this regard; it becomes easy to spread messages, to carry the meaning of different contexts and to convey important messages throughout the organization. Stories and storytelling can directly influence the attributes and characteristics of organizational members by promoting resilience and fostering commitment. Storytelling is a thought-provoking and collaborative process that can be used successfully to implement changes in the organization. Storytelling can motivate employees. It can provide more ways through which an effective change can be implemented in the organization.

Storytelling is a frequent tool among companies aiming to create a connection between leaders and their teams. Storytelling is the oldest way of telling stories.

Storytelling favors the understanding of complex issues and helps translate strategy into action. This permits professionals to have an in-depth and clear idea about their objectives and the company, which is important and essential in generating their identities and purpose.

The organizational narrative has both an individual and collective role: on one hand, it serves to make the individual feel part of a culture that believes in and can make important contributions.

Dr. Radisha Brown

The other is an active tool of communication and engagement, able to convey an inspiring message.

Through stories, lessons from the past begin to make sense and the future possibilities become clearer. In companies, the tool can manifest itself in various ways, through strategic decisions, values, business practices, and ways of addressing stakeholders, among others.

Storytelling is a set of communication techniques that have existed since language evolved some 30 to 100 thousand years ago. These techniques consist of organizing facts in a sequence, for reasons explained by human psychology, neurology and even anthropology. They have the power to give new meanings to information.

Therefore, every organization, since its inception, now has an identity…becomes part of a story. This story is constructed from a range of experiences and visions related to internal and external relations of their daily events. When connected to a professional organization that offers a product or service to a customer, giving examples and telling stories is a technique called storytelling. This technique uses the stories and narratives as a tool for communication and education, favoring results.

But the storytelling technique is useful for presenting organizations in modern times, also. We live in a society where information is increasingly abundant, and people's attention is increasingly scarce. There is the impression that we walked into a rhythm of life that makes it feel impossible to monitor everything

The Art of Storytelling

215| P a g e

that happens around us and the world.

The longstanding mode of storytelling is an innovative form of communication that is used by various organizations and can also be used by any professional, in various situations such as meetings, personal conversations, public presentations, negotiations or sales. The professional can engage your customers, your staff, your employees and partners through an open form of communication.

The power of narratives and histories, internal and external communication, is becoming a more effective way to interact, motivate, become close, be empathetic and practice otherness in the corporate world. In other words, telling a good story is the shortest way to get someone's attention.

Although that may seem quiet and easy, the gift of creating a story that really attracts the attention of your viewers is a complex process. It requires a large investment of time, which is already an increasingly scarce element in our society.

The support of management in the process and efforts to bring change is an important component in establishing the readiness for change. Researchers have predicted that the extent to which the practices and policies of the organization support change is also an essential factor in determining the ways in which the organization's employees perceive the change. This includes the support systems, logistics, and flexibility in procedures and policies. Additionally, the trust level among employees and management can promote the perception of whether the organization can handle the change.

The change in support is also reflected in the leadership. A strong leadership includes change monitoring, making required amendments, initiating creative visions when needed. Managing and leading the change require the leaders to have the learning capability to adapt and learn from the changes. In this procedure, the learning process of the organizations is promoted within an environment of mutual trust and openness which permits individuals to accept changes and experiment without feeling threatened.

One form of management support toward an organization's change effort can be reflected by forming an exceptional team. The team is responsible to conduct analysis toward influencing internal and external conditions, plan change process in more detail, identify possible risks and anticipated actions, and to control implementation, including progress evaluation and conduct adjustment toward the real situation.

Management support can also be reflected from how change is accommodated by management through realignment of performance evaluation and employee compensation within the change initiative program. Change demands sacrifice from the employee. During the change process, the employee will feel uncomfortable with the new surroundings. Thus, sacrifice, participation, and commitment from members of organizations must be rewarded through performance evaluation and compensation.

To conclude, it can be said that, organizational change is a 360-degree process which requires a commitment to the processes, effective leadership, cultural change management, and timely evaluations. The organizations that are not receptive to the internal and external changes may become extinct. Survival of the fittest theory applies here in the same way as social life. To survive, businesses need to adopt to an ever changing world.

Dr. Radisha Brown

The Art of Storytelling

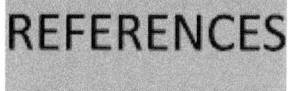

# REFERENCES

Abrahamson, E. 2000. Change without pain. *Harvard Business Review* (July-August): 75-79.

Adamson, G., Pine, J., van Steenhoven, T., & Kroupa, J. (2006) How storytelling can drive strategic change. Strategy & Leadership, 34(1), 36 – 41.

Albert, S., Ashford, B., & Dutton, J. (2000). *Academy of Management Review, 25*, 13-17.

Anderson, C. (1997). Values-based management. *Academy of Management Executive.*
*11*, 25-46.

Anfuso, D. (1998). Stories communicate Red Robin's culture. *Workforce, 77*, 41. Appelbaum, E. T., Bailey T., Berg P., & Kalleberg, A. (2000) *Manufacturing advantage:*
*why high-performance work systems pay off.* Ithaca: ILR Press.

Auvinen, T. P., Aaltio, I. E., & Blomqvist, K. (2013). Constructing leadership by storytelling–the meaning of trust and narratives. *Leadership & Organization Development Journal, 34*(6), 1-1.

Axelrod, R. H. (2002). *Terms of engagement: Changing the way we change organizations.* San Francisco: Berrett-Koehler Publishers.

Barker, R. T., & Gower, K. (2010). Strategic application of storytelling in organizations toward effective communication in a diverse world. *Journal of Business Communication, 47*(3), p. 2-12, retrieved from http://job.sagepub.com/content/47/3/295.short

Barney, J. (1991). Firm resources and sustained competitive advantage. *Journal of Management, 17*, 99-120.

Battilana, J., & Tiziana, C. (2012). Change agents, networks, and institutions: A contingency theory of organizational change. *Academy of Management Journal* 55(2), (April 2012).

Dr. Radisha Brown

Beer M., & Nohria, N. (2000). *Breaking the code of change.* Boston Massachusetts: Harvard Business School Press.

Berman, D., & Oleck, J. (1998). Calling all raconteurs. Business Week, 3602: 6.

Best, J., & Kahn, J. (2006). *Research in education* (8th ed.). Boston: Allyn and Bacon. Blundel, R., & Ippolito, K. (2008). *Effective organizational communication: perspectives, principles, and practices.* New York: Pearson Education.

Boal, K. B., & Schultz, P. L. (2007). Storytelling, time, and evolution: The role of strategic leadership in complex adaptive systems. *The Leadership Quarterly, 18*(4), p. 3-6, retrieved from http://www.sciencedirect.com/science/article/pii/S1048984307000744

Borgatti, S. (2011), Introduction to grounded theory. Retrieved from http://www.analytictech.com/mb870/introtogt.htm

Boje, D. (1991). The storytelling organization: A study of story performance in an office- supply firm. *Administrative Science Quarterly, 36*, 106-126.

Boje, D. (1995). Stories of the storytelling organization: A postmodern analysis of Disney as "Tamara-land." *Academy of Management Journal, 38*(4), 997-1035.

Boje, D., Luhman, J., & Baack, D. (1999). Hegemonic stories and encounters between storytelling organizations. *Journal of Management Inquiry, 8*, 340-360.

Bowman, G., MacKay, R. B., Masrani, S., & McKiernan, P. (2013). Storytelling and the scenario process: Understanding success and failure. *Technological Forecasting and Social Change, 80*(4), 3-15. retrieved from http://www.sciencedirect.com/science/article/pii/S0040162512000984

Boyce. M. (1996). Organizational story and storytelling: A Critical Review. *Journal of Organizational Change Management, 9*(5), 5-26.

Breuer, N. (1998). The power of storytelling. *Workforce, 77*, 36-41.

Bridges, W. (1994). *Job Shift: How to prosper in a workplace without jobs.* Reading, MA: Addison-Wesley.

Broom, A., & Willis, E. (2007). *Competing paradigms and health research.* London: Sage Publications. Data retrieved from http://www.sagepub.com/upm- data/13614_02_Saks_ch02.pdf

The Art of Storytelling

Brower, R. S., & Abolafia, M. Y. (1995). The structural embeddedness of resistance among public managers. *Group and Organization Management, 20*, 149-166.

Brown, M. (1990). *Defining stories in organizations: Characteristics and functions.* In J.A. Anderson (Ed.), *Communication Yearbook, 13*, 162-190. Newbury Park, CA: Sage.

Brown, M., & Kreps, G. (1993). Narrative analysis and organizational development. In S. Herndon, & G. Kreps, (Eds.), *Qualitative research: Applications in organizational communication.* Cresskill. NJ: Hampton Press.

Brusoni, S., & Rosenkranz, N. A. (2014). Reading between the lines: Learning as a process between organizational context and individuals' proclivities. *European Management Journal*, 32(1): 147-154.

Buchanan, M. (2013). Time to think. *Nature Physics,* 752-752.

Buckner, K.A., & Wakefield, M. (2006). Leading in the times of change. *Harvard Management, 3,* 2-10.

Buhanist, P. (2000). *Organisational change, development efforts, and action research.* Doctoral Dissertation. Helsinki, University of Technology.

Burnes, B., & Cooke, B. (2013). Kurt Lewin's field theory: A review and re-evaluation. International Journal of Management Reviews, 15(4), 408-425.

Burns, N., & Grove, S. (2007). *Understanding nursing research: Building evidence-based practice.* (4th ed.). St. Louis, MO: Saunders, Elsevier Inc.

Caelli, K. (2002). Quantitative and qualitative research: Competition or parallel play?
*Journal of Wound, Ostomy and Continence Nursing, 29*(2), 74-75. Data retrieved from http://www.ncbi.nlm.nih.gov/pubmed/11901414

Carriger, M. (2010). The function of narrative in leadership: Theoretical foundations and empirical evidence. Unpub. Diss., University of Maryland University College,

Carson, P., Carson, K., & Lanier, P. (2001). The stainless steel career: An examination of workplace resilience. *The Journal of Applied Management and Entrepreneurship, 6*(2), 3-13.

Dr. Radisha Brown

Choi, M., & Ruona, W. (2010). Individual readiness for organizational change and its implications for human resource and organization development. *Human Resource Development Review, 3,* 46-73.

Collins, J. (2001). *Good to great: Why some companies make the leap...and others don't.* New York: Harper Business.

Collins, J., & Porras, J. (1994). *Built to last: Successful habits of visionary companies.* New York: Harper Business.

Collins, K. M. T., Onwuegbuzie, A. J., & Jiao, Q. G. (2006). Prevalence of mixed methods sampling designs in social science research and beyond. Paper presented at the meeting of the American Educational Research Association, San Francisco.

Conner, D. (1998). How to create a nimble organization. *National Productivity Review, 17*(4), 31-36.

Cooke, M. (1992) Computer analyses of qualitative data: A literature review of current issues. *Australian Journal of Advanced Nursing, 10*(1), 10-13.

Creswell, J. W. (2008). *Research design: Qualitative, quantitative, and mixed methods approaches.* 3rd edition. Los Angeles CA: Sage.

Cullen, J. (2008). Catalyzing innovation and knowledge sharing: Librarian 2.0. *Business Information Review, 3,* 253-258.

Cummings, T. G., & Worley, C. G. (1993). *Organisation development and change.* 5$^{th}$ edition. St Paul (MN): West Publishing Company.

Dahl, M. S. (2011). Organizational change and employee stress. *Management Science, 57*(2), 240-256.

Dailey, S., & Browning, L. (2013). Retelling stories in organizations: Understanding the functions of narrative repetition. *Academy of Management Review, 4,* 3-10.

Dennehy, R. (1999). The executive as storyteller. *Management Review, 88,* 40-43.

Denning, S. (2010). *The leader's guide to radical management reinventing the workplace for the 21st Century.* San Francisco: Jossey-Bass.

Doe, P. (1994). Creating a resilient organization. *Canadian Business Review, 21*(2), 22.

The Art of Storytelling

Down, J., & King, J. (1999). Towards a science of stories: Implications for management education. *Proceedings of the Academy of Management Annual Conference, 19,* 1-4. Chicago, IL.

Egan, G., & Egan, G. (2010). *Exercises in helping skills: A manual to accompany the skilled helper, a problem-management and opportunity-development approach to helping,* (9th ed.). Australia: Brooks/Cole, Cengage Learning.

Earl, M. (1989). *Management strategies for information technology.* New York: Prentice Hall.

Eccles, R., Nohria, N., & Berkley, J. (1992). *Beyond the hype: Rediscovering the essence of management.* Boston MA: Harvard Business School Press.

Erwin, D. G., & Garman, A. N. (2010). Resistance to organizational change: Linking research and practice. *Leadership & Organization Development Journal, 31*(1), 39 – 56.

Festing, M. (2012). State of the art: International human resource management and cultural learning. *Global Collaboration: Intercultural Experiences and Learning,* 3-14. Retrieved from http://books.google.com.pk/books?hl=en&lr=&id=SXSaErsJPGEC&oi= fnd&pg= PA59&dq=storytelling+in+companies++human+resourc+manaement +and+comm unication&ots=riLrZbXv5Y&sig=8zXbU8jSUGmdLsoijckxpiwQY9E

Fine, S. (1991). Resilience and human adaptability: Who rises to adversity? *American Journal of Occupational Therapy, 45,* 493 -503.

Fiol, C. (1994). Consensus, diversity, and learning in organizations. *Organization Science, 5,* 21-50.

Ford, J. D., Ford, L. W., & McNamara, R. T. (2002). Resistance and the background conversations of change. *Journal of Organizational Change Management, 15*(2), 5-15.

Fugate, M., Prussia, G.E., & Kinicki, A. J. (2012). Managing employee withdrawal during organizational change: The role of threat appraisal. *Journal of Management,* 38, 890-914.

Gardner, H., & Laskin, E. (1995). *Leading minds: An anatomy of leadership.* New York, NY: BasicBooks.

Geiger, D., & Schreyögg, G. (2012). Narratives in knowledge sharing: challenging validity. *Journal of Knowledge Management, 16*(1), 10-18. Retrieved from http://www.emeraldinsight.com/journals.htm?articleid=17015624&show=abstract

Geller, E. S. (2002). The challenge of increasing pro-environmental behavior. In R. B. Bechtel, & A. Churchman (Eds.), *Handbook of environmental psychology* (pp. 525–540). New York: Wiley.

Gersick, C., Bartunek, J., & Dutton, J. (2000). Learning from academia: The importance of relationships in professional life. *Academy of Management Journal, 43*(6), 1026-1044.

Gill, R. (2011). Using storytelling to maintain employee loyalty during change.*International Journal of Business and Social Science, 2*(1), 6-23. Retrieved from http://www.ijbssnet.com/journals/Vol_2_No_15_August_2011/4.pdf

Gioia, D., Schultz, M., & Corley, K. (2000). Organizational identity, image, and adaptive instability. *Academy of Management Review, 25*, 63-81.

Goldkuhl, G. (2012). Pragmatism vs interpretivism in qualitative information systems research. *European Journal of Information Systems, 21*(2), 135–146. doi:10.1057/ ejis.2011.54

Goodstein, L. D., & Burke, W.W. (1997). Creating successful organization change. In C.A. Carnall, (Ed.), *Strategic change* (pp. 159-173). Oxford: Butterworth- Heinemann.

Gotsill, G., & Natchez, M. (2007). From resistance to acceptance: How to implement change management. *T+D, 61*(11), 24-27.

Griffin, R., & Moorhead, G. (2011). *Organizational behavior: Managing people and organizations* (10th ed.). Mason, OH: South-Western/Cengage Learning.

Hall, D. (1994). The new "career contract": Wrong on both counts. Boston: Executive Development Roundtable, Boston University School of Management, Report #9403.

Hall, D. T., & Mirvis, P. H. (1996). The new protean career: Psychological success and the path with a heart. In D. T. Hall (Ed.), *The career is dead – long live the career*: 15–45. San Francisco: Jossey-Bass.

Hall, D., & Moss, J. (1998). *The new protean career contract: How organizations and employees adapt.* Organizational Dynamics, Winter.

Hannabuss, S. (1996). Research interviews. *New Library World, 97*(5), 22 – 30. Harenstam, A., Bejerot, E., Leijon, O., Sche´ele, K., & Waldenstrom, K. (2004). Multilevel analyses of organizational change and working conditions in public and private sector. *European Journal of Work and Organizational Psychology, 13*(3), 305–43.

Harris, J., & Barnes, B. K. (2006). Leadership storytelling. *Industrial and Commercial Training, 38*(7), 5-16.
Haveman, H. A., Russo, M. V., & Meyer, A. D. (2001). Organizational environments in flux: The impact for regulatory punctuations on organizational domains, CEO succession, and performance. *Organization Science, 12,* 253-273.

Hearn, G., Foth, M., & Gray, H. (2009). Applications and implementations of new media in corporate communications: An action research approach. *Corporate Communications: An International Journal, 14*(1), 49-61.

Heckscher, C. (1995). *White Collar Blues: Management Loyalties in an Age of Corporate Restructuring.* New York: Basic Books.

Hildebrand, J. (1998). *Bridging the gap: A training module in personal and professional development.* London: Karnac Books.

Hirschhorn, L. (2000), Changing structure is not enough: The moral meaning of organizational design. In M. Beer & N. Nohria (Eds.), *Breaking the code of change* (pp. 161-176). Boston MA: Harvard Business School.

Hollenbeck, G., & McCall, M. (1998). Leadership development: Contemporary practice. In A. Kraut, & A. Korman (Eds.), *Changing concepts and practices for human resource management: Contributions from Industrial/Organizational Psychology.* San Francisco: Jossey-Bass.

Home, J., & Orr, J. (1998). Assessing behaviors that create resilient organizations. *Employment Relations Today, 24*(4), 29-39.

Hoopes, L. (1999). Team resilience. *Executive Excellence, 16*(5), 16.

Jarvenpaa, E., & Eloranta, E. (2000). Organizational culture and organizational development. In W. Karwowski (Ed.), *International encyclopedia of ergonomics and human factors.* New York: Taylor and Francis Inc.

Johansson, C., & Heide, M. (2008). Speaking of change: Three communication approaches in studies of organizational change. *Corporate Communications: An International Journal, 13*(3), 288-305.

Dr. Radisha Brown

Johnson, R. B., & Onwuegbuzie, A. J. (2004). Mixed methods research: A research paradigm whose time has come. *Educational Researcher, 33*(7), 14-26.

Johnson, B., Onwuegbuzie, A., & Turner, L. (2007). Toward a definition of mixed methods research. *Journal of Mixed Methods Research, 1*, 112-133.

Jones, G. R. (2004). *Organization theory, design, and change.* New York: Addison- Wesley Publishing Company.

Jones, G. (2010). *Organizational theory, design, and change: Text and cases* (5th ed.). Upper Saddle River, NJ: Pearson Prentice Hall.

Kalliath, T. Bluedom, A., & Strube, M. (1999). A test of value congruence effects. *Journal of Organizational Behavior, 20*, 1175-1198.

Kankainen, A., Vaajakallio, K., Kantola, V., & Mattelmäki, T. (2012). Storytelling Group–a co-design method for service design. *Behaviour & Information Technology, 31*(3), 221-230.

Kanter, R. M. (1995). *World class: Thriving locally in the global economy.* New York: Touchstone Books.

Karkabi, K., Wald, H. S., & Castel, O. C. (2013). The use of abstract paintings and narratives to foster reflective capacity in medical educators: A multinational faculty development workshop. *Medical Humanities*, 4-16. Retrieved from http://www.thejournalofbusiness.org/index.php/site/article/view/55

Kachel, U., & Jennings, G. (2010). Exploring tourists' environmental learning, values and travel experiences in relation to climate change: A postmodern constructivist research agenda. *Tourism & Hospitality Research, 10*(2), 130–140. doi:10.1057/ thr.2009.34

Kaye, B., & Jacobson, B. (1999). True tales and tall tales: The power of organizational storytelling. *Training and Development, 5*, 44-50.

Kearney, M. (2011). A learning design for student-generated digital storytelling. *Learning, Media, and Technology, 36*(2), 169-188.

Ketchen, D., Boyd, B.K., & Bergh, D.D. (2008). Research methods in strategic management: Past accomplishments and future challenges. *Organizational Research Methods, 11*, 643-658.

Kirk, J., & Miller, M. (1986). *Reliability and validity in qualitative research.* Beverly Hills: Sage Publications.

Kotter, J. (1996). *Leading change.* Boston MA: Harvard Business School.

Kotter, J. P., & Cohen, D. S. (2002). *The heart of change: Real-life stories of how people change their organizations.* Boston MA: Harvard Business School Press.

Kouzes, J., & Posner, B. (1995). *The leadership challenge.* San Francisco CA: Jossey- Bass.

Kreps, G. (1990). Stories as repositories of organizational intelligence: Implications for organizational development. In J. A. Anderson (Ed.), *Communication Yearbook* (pp. 191-202). Newbury Park, CA: Sage.

Kumar, M. (2007). Mixed methodology research design in educational technology. *Alberta Journal of Educational Research, 53*(1), 34-44.

LeBow, R., & Simon, W. (1997). *Lasting change: The shared values process that makes companies great.* New York: Van Nostrand Reinhold/ITP.

London. M. (1983). Toward a theory of career motivation. *Academy of Management Review, 8,* 620-630.

London, M., & Mone, E.M. (1987). *Career management and survival in the workplace.* San Francisco: Jossey-Bass.

Louis, M., & Sutton, R. (1991). Switching cognitive gears: From habits of mind to active thinking. *Human Relations, 44,* 55-76.

Love, H. (2008). Unraveling the technique of storytelling. *Strategic Communication Management, 12*(4), 24-27.

McCall. M. (1998). *High fivers: Developing the next generation of leaders.* Boston MA: Harvard Business.

McCarthy, J. (1999). Talking through tough times: Organizational short stories at Wilhelmsen Lines. Proceedings of the Institute for Behavioral and Applied Management 1999 Annual Conference. Annapolis, MD.

McCarthy, J., & Hall. D. T. (2000). Organizational crisis and change: The new career contract at work. In R. Burke & C. Cooper, C. (Eds.), *The organization in crisis: downsizing, restructuring, and privatization.* London: Blackwell Publishers.

McCarthy, J. F. (2008). Short stories at work: Storytelling as an indicator of organizational commitment. *Group & Organization Management,* 33(2), 163-193.

Dr. Radisha Brown

McCollom, M. (1991a). *Organizational stories in a family-owned business: Reflections of the system dynamics.* Boston University Working Paper Series, 91-23. Boston: Boston University Publications.

McCollom, M. (1991b). *Saga and the (re)construction of organizational history.* Boston University Working Paper Series, 91-17. Boston: Boston University Publications.

McCollom, M. (1991c). *Story or saga? Narrative form and organizational change.* Boston University Working Paper Series, 91-25. Boston: Boston University Publications.

Mauthner, M., Birch, M., Jessop, J., & Miller, T. (2003). *Ethics in qualitative research.* London: Sage Publications.

Meyer, J., & Allen, N. (1991). A three-component conceptualization of organizational commitment. *Human Resource Management Review, 1,* 61-89.

Meyer, J., & Allen, N. (1997). *Commitment in the workplace: Theory, research, and application.* Thousand Oaks, CA: Sage.

Mirvis, P., & Marks, M. (1992). *Managing the merger: Making it work.* Englewood Cliffs. NJ: Prentice Hall.

Mittins, M., Abratt, R., & Christie, P. (2011). Storytelling in reputation management: the case of Nashua Mobile South Africa. *Management Decision, 49*(3), 405-421. Retrieved from http://www.emeraldinsight.com/journals.htm?articleid=1913471&show=abstract

Mládková, L. (2012). Sharing tacit knowledge within organizations: Evidence from the Czech Republic. *Global Journal of Business Research, 6*(2).

Morgan, G. (1997). *Images of organization.* Thousand Oaks, CA: Sage.

Mowday, R,, Steers, R., & Porter. L. (1979). The measurement of organizational commitment. *Journal of Vocational Behavior, 14,* 224-247.

Neuhauser, P. (1993). *Corporate legends and lore: The power of storytelling as a management tool.* New York: McGraw-Hill.

Nkomo, S., & Cox, T. (1996). Diverse identities in organizations. In S.R. Clegg, C. Hardy & W.R. Nord (Eds), *Handbook of organization studies, pp. 312-315,* London: Sage.

The Art of Storytelling

Nonas, K. (2005). *Vision versus reality in organizational change*. Stockholm: National Institute for Working Life.

O'Cathain, A., Murphy, E., & Nicholl, J. (2007). Integration and publications as indicators of yield from mixed methods studies. *Journal of Mixed Methods Research, 1*, 147-163.

O'Leary, R., Choi, Y., & Gerard, C. (2012). The Skill Set of the Successful Collaborator.*Public Administration Review Public Admin Rev.* doi: 10.1111/j.1540- 6210.2012.02667.x

O'Toole, J. (1995). *Leading change: Overcoming the ideology of comfort and the tyranny of custom.* San Francisco, CA: Jossey-Bass.

Oreg, S., & Sverdlik, N. (2011). Ambivalence toward imposed change: The conflict between dispositional resistance to change and the orientation toward the change agent. *Journal of Applied Psychology, 3,* 337-349.

Oreg, S., Vakola, M., & Armenakis, A. (2011). Change recipients' reactions to organizational change: A 60-year review of quantitative studies. *The Journal of Applied Behavioral Science, 3,* 461-524.

Paine, L. (1994). Managing for organizational integrity. *Harvard Business Review,*(March–April 1994

Pfeffermann, N. (2011). Innovation communication as a cross-functional dynamic capability: Strategies for organizations and networks. In *Strategies and communications for innovations* (pp. 257-289). Berlin Heidelberg: Springer.

Piderit, S. K. (2000). Rethinking resistance and recognizing ambivalence: A multidimensional view of attitudes toward an organizational change. *Academy of Management Review, 25*(4), 783-794.

Poole, M. S., & Van de Ven, A. H. (2004). *Handbook of organizational change and innovation.* Oxford: Oxford University Press.

Powell, S., Elving, W. J., Dodd, C., & Sloan, J. (2009). Explicating ethical corporate identity in the financial sector. *Corporate Communications: An International Journal, 14*(4), 440-455.

Pratt, M., & Foreman, P. (2000). Classifying managerial responses to multiple identities. *Academy of Management Review, 25,* 18-42.

Pulley, M. (1997). *Losing your job - Reclaiming your soul: Stories of resilience, renewal, and hope.* San Francisco CA: Jossey-Bass.

Dr. Radisha Brown

Ramer, A. (1997). *Revelations for a new millennium*. San Francisco CA: Harper.

Ribiere, V. M., & Sitar, A. S. (2003). Critical role of leadership in nurturing a knowledge-supporting culture. *Knowledge Management Research & Practice*, 1(1), 10-21.

Rosile, G. A., Boje, D. M., Carlon, D. M., Downs, A., & Saylors, R. (2013). Storytelling diamond: An ante-narrative integration of the six facets of storytelling in organization research design. *Organizational Research Methods*, 4-12. Retrieved from http://orm.sagepub.com/content/early/2013/04/22/1094428113482490.abstract

Rousseau, D. (1995). *The psychological contract in organizations*. Thousand Oaks, CA: Sage.

Rousseau, D. (1998). Why workers still identify with organizations. *Journal of Organizational Behavior, 19,* 217-233.

Salminen, A.(2000). *Implementing organizational and operational change – Critical success factors of change management*. Unpub doctoral dissertation, Helsinki University of Technology, Executive School of Industrial Management.

Schank, R. (1990). *Tell me a story: Narrative and intelligence*. Evanston, IL: Northwestern University Press.

Senge, P. (1990). *The fifth discipline: The art & practice of the learning organization*. New York: Currency Doubleday.

Seo, M., Taylor, M., Hill, N., Zhang, X., Tesluk, P., & Lorinkova, N. (2012). The role of affect and leadership during organizational change. *Personnel Psychology*, 65(1), 121-165.

Senior, B., & Fleming, J. (2006). *Organizational change*. Esse: Pearson Education Limited.

Shaw, R., Ramachandra, V., Lucas, N., & Robinson, N. (1998). *Essentials for Doctors*. Cambridge: Cambridge University Press.

Shields, J. (1999). Transforming organizations, methods for accelerating culture change processes. *Information Knowledge Systems Management, 1*(2), 105-115 (April).

Siders, M., George, G., & Dharwadkar, R. (2001). The relationship of internal and external commitment foci to objective job performance measures. *The Academy of Management Journal, 44*(3), 570-579.

The Art of Storytelling

Seidman, I. (2006). *Interviewing as qualitative research: A guide for researchers in education and the social sciences* (3rd ed.). New York, NY. Teachers College Press.

Silverman, D. (2006). *Interpreting qualitative data: Methods for analyzing talk, text, and interaction* (3rd ed.). London: SAGE Publications.

Smissen, S., Schalk, R., & Freese, C. (2013). Organizational change and the psychological contract. *Journal of Organizational Change Management,* 3, 1071- 1090.

Sole, D., & Wilson, D. G. (2002). Storytelling in organizations: The power and traps of using stories to share knowledge in organizations. Harvard LILA *Graduate School of Education,* 3-7.

Stanley, D. J., Meyer, J. P., & Topolnytsky, L. (2005). Employee cynicism and resistance to organizational change. *Journal of Business & Psychology, 19*(4), 429-459.

Stewart, A. (1998). *The ethnographer's method.* Thousand Oaks, Calif.: Sage Publications.

Taylor-Powell, E., & Renner, M. (2003). *Analyzing qualitative data.* Learning Store, University of Wisconsin. Retrieved April 7, 2015, from http://learningstore.uwex.edu/assets/pdfs/G3658-12.PDF

Thomas, R., Sargent, L., & Hardy, C. (2011). Managing organizational change: Negotiating meaning and power-resistance relations. *Organization Science, 22*(1), 22-41.

Tichy, N., & Cardwell, N. (2002). *The cycle of leadership: How great leaders teach their companies to win.* New York, NY: Harper Business.

Tobin, P. K., & Snyman, R. (2008, March). Once upon a time in Africa: A case study of storytelling for knowledge sharing. *Aslib Proceedings, 60*(2) 130-142. Emerald Group Publishing Limited.

Trimble, J. (2006). *The handbook of ethical research with ethnocultural populations and communities.* Thousand Oaks, CA: Sage Publications.

van Vuuren, M., & Elving, W. J. (2008). Communication, sensemaking, and change as a chord of three strands: Practical implications and a research agenda for communicating organizational change. *Corporate Communications: An International Journal, 13*(3), 349-359.

Varga, A. M. (2012). Best practices in employee communications: Clarity, community, context, convergence, and customization. p. 4-15. Retrieved from http://annmarievarga.com/wp-content/uploads/2013/02/Best-Practices-in-Employee-Communications.pdf

Dr. Radisha Brown

Venkitachalam, K., & Busch, P. (2012). Tacit knowledge: review and possible research directions. *Journal of Knowledge Management, 16*(2), p. 5-15.

Volkoff, O., & Strong, D. (2013). Critical realism and affordances: Theorizing IT- associated organizational change processes. *MIS Quarterly, 37*(3), 819-834.

Wanberg, C.R., & Banas, J.T. (2000). Predictors and outcomes of openness to changes in a reorganizing workplace. *Journal of Applied Psychology, 85,* 132-142.

Weick, K. (1995). *Sensemaking in organizations.* Thousand Oaks: Sage Publications.

Whyte, G., & Classen, S. (2012). Using storytelling to elicit tacit knowledge from SMEs. *Journal of Knowledge Management, 16*(6), 950-962. Retrieved from http://www.emeraldinsight.com/journals.htm?articleid=17062895&show=abstract

Yang, R. S., Zhuo, X. Z., & Yu, H. Y. (2009). *Organization theory and management: cases, measurements, and industrial applications.* Taipei: Yeh-Yeh Press.

# APPENDIX A

**Interview Questions**

Dr. Radisha Brown

## APPENDIX A

### Interview Questions

1. Can you explain what is storytelling?

2. Can you describe what you believe are the important features of storytelling?

3. What has been your experience with your organization using storytelling to communicate organizational change?

4. Describe your feelings about organizations using storytelling to communicate change?

5. Tell me what you think about storytelling encouraging full engagement of employees?

6. What advice would you give your leader about using storytelling to communicate organizational change?

# APPENDIX B

## Informed Consent

**APPENDIX B**

**Informed Consent**

# USING STORYTELLING AS A COMMUNICATION TOOL

## Purpose of the Study:

This survey explores the phenomenon of organizational storytelling, where stories serve to convey meaning and to pass on values in organizations, linking the organization's members more tightly with each other - and with their leaders.

## Interview

During the interview, you will be asked to answer questions about your beliefs about leaders using storytelling to communicate organizational change. You will be asked six interview questions at which time the researcher will transcribe your responses. The interview will take approximately 60 minutes to complete.

## Benefits of this Study

You will be contributing to knowledge about the use of storytelling and organizational leadership.

## Confidentiality:

Your responses will be kept completely confidential. All information will remain strictly confidential and will be recorded without your name.

## Decision to quit at any time:

Your participation is voluntary; you are free to withdraw your participation from this study at any time. If you do not want to continue, you can simply ask for the interview to be discontinued. If you choose to form the research your response will not be recorded.

## How the findings will be used:

The results of the study will be used for scholarly purposes only. The results from the study will be presented in educational settings, professional conferences, or the results could be published in a professional journal in the field of business or psychology.

## Contact information:

If you have concerns or questions about this study, please contact Radisha Brown at radishabrown@gmail.com or Argosy University's Research Review Board.

_____

Participant's Signature          Date

The Art of Storytelling

Dr. Radisha Brown is the founder and CEO of TLC Services, an online mental health practice that provides counseling services by video, telephone or text message 4pm-midnight Monday-Friday and by appointment on the weekends. Dr. Radisha launched this online practice to provide an opportunity for individuals to obtain mental health services with a licensed professional therapist right from the comfort of their home or office.

Dr. Radisha grew up in South Carolina. She was the first person in her family to attend college and she received her bachelor's degree in sociology with a minor in Social Work from Augusta State University in Augusta, GA. Dr. Radisha went on to receive her master's degree in social work from the University of South Carolina in Columbia, South Carolina and then she went on to complete her doctorate degree in business with a focus on leadership from Argosy University in Atlanta, Ga.

Dr. Radisha spent over ten years of corporate business experience in addition to her experience in providing mental health services to adults and children. She combines her clinical counseling expertise with her business knowledge; to offer a unique perspective on problem-solving to help clients achieve positive changes in their life.

www.Talk2TLC.com

Facebook  @drradisha brown      @Talk2TLC

The Art of Storytelling

www.ingramcontent.com/pod-product-compliance
Lightning Source LLC
Chambersburg PA
CBHW061505180526
45171CB00001B/38